Tourism and Nati

Identity

TOURISM AND CULTURAL CHANGE

Series Editors: Professor Mike Robinson, *Ironbridge International Institute for Cultural Heritage, Univer ty of Birmingham, UK* and Dr Alison Phipps, *University of Glasgow, Scotland, UK*

TCC is a series of books that explores the complex and ever-changing relationship between tourism and culture(s). The series focuses on the ways that places, peoples, pasts, and ways of life are increasingly shaped/transformed/created/packaged for touristic purposes. The series examines the ways tourism utilises/makes and re-makes cultural capital in its various guises (visual and performing arts, crafts, festivals, built heritage, cuisine, etc.) and the multifarious political, economic, social and ethical issues that are raised as a consequence.

Understanding tourism's relationships with culture(s) and vice versa, is of ever-increasing significance in a globalising world. This series will critically examine the dynamic inter-relationships between tourism and culture(s). Theoretical explorations, research-informed analyses and detailed historical reviews from a variety of disciplinary perspectives are invited to consider such relationships.

Full details of all the books in this series and of all our other publications can be found on http://www.channelviewpublications.com, or by writing to Channel View Publications, St Nicholas House, 31–34 High Street, Bristol BS1 2AW, UK.

TOURISM AND CULTURAL CHANGE: 39

Tourism and National Identity

Heritage and Nationhood in Scotland

Kalyan Bhandari

CHANNEL VIEW PUBLICATIONS
Bristol • Buffalo • Toronto

Library of Congress Cataloging in Publication Data
Bhandari, Kalyan, 1975-
Tourism and National Identity : Heritage and Nationhood in Scotland/Kalyan Bhandari.
Tourism and Cultural Change: 39
Includes bibliographical references and index.
1. Tourism—Social aspects—Scotland. 2. Heritage tourism—Scotland. 3. National characteristics, Scottish. I. Title.
G155.G7B53 2014
338.4'791411–dc23 2014003188

British Library Cataloguing in Publication Data
A catalogue entry for this book is available from the British Library.

ISBN-13: 978-1-84541-448-1 (hbk)
ISBN-13: 978-1-84541-447-4 (pbk)

Channel View Publications
UK: St Nicholas House, 31–34 High Street, Bristol BS1 2AW, UK.
USA: UTP, 2250 Military Road, Tonawanda, NY 14150, USA.
Canada: UTP, 5201 Dufferin Street, North York, Ontario M3H 5T8, Canada.

Website: www.channelviewpublications.com
Twitter: Channel_View
Facebook: https://www.facebook.com/channelviewpublications
Blog: www.channelviewpublications.wordpress.com

The policy of Multilingual Matters/Channel View Publications is to use papers that are natural, renewable and recyclable products, made from wood grown in sustainable forests. In the manufacturing process of our books, and to further support our policy, preference is given to printers that have FSC and PEFC Chain of Custody certification. The FSC and/or PEFC logos will appear on those books where full certification has been granted to the printer concerned.

Typeset by Techset Composition India(P) Ltd., Bangalore and Chennai, India.
Printed and bound in Great Britain by Short Run Press Ltd.

Contents

Illustrations

Figures

Acknowledgements

I owe heartfelt thanks to many people for their help and support in writing this book: most of all to Dr Donald Macleod and Professor Ted Cowan from the University of Glasgow who were the first readers of the materials when I originally prepared this work for my doctoral thesis. They provided me with their continuous supervision, intellectual support, valuable comments and regular feedback throughout my doctoral research and have continued to do so. I am also indebted to all staff members at the School of Interdisciplinary Studies, University of Glasgow in Dumfries where I was a doctoral student until 2012.

Since then I have moved to two other institutions. I thank everyone at Oxford Brookes University's Business School where I worked as a Post-doctoral Research Assistant on a climate change research project. This work gave me new insight into tourism and organisational adaptation, which was a very different perspective from the one I was familiar with. It was at Brookes that I began working on this book and Professor Chris Cooper made sure that I had an excellent environment and support while working there. Chris was a great mentor, an ideal person any new researcher like me would want to work with. I would like to thank him for his help, support and encouragement. I would also like to thank the following colleagues at Brookes: Dr Victoria Waligo, Dr Peter Lugosi, Professor Levent Altinay and Donald Sloan.

Since finishing my project at Oxford Brookes, I have moved back to Scotland to a new position at the University of the West of Scotland (UWS). I thank the entire team at the UWS's Events and Tourism subject group for ensuring that I settled in well and for providing me with the help that I needed to continue with my book project. I would like to thank Ron Livingston and Siobhan Drummond for taking care of everything at UWS. Other colleagues at UWS I would like to thank are: Heather Anderson, Tom Garrett, Stephen Edinborough, Jacqui Greener, Brenda Hughes and Alan Murray.

This study would not have been possible without the help of people who responded to my research. It is not possible to name them all but some of them cannot go unmentioned. They are: Madam May McKerrell of The Border Gathering, Lez Byers of Ellisland Farm, Ian McClumpha and Doug Archibald of the The Bruce Trust, and Cathy Gibb from Dumfries and Galloway Archive. I thank them all. Additionally, I would also like to thank the following individuals for help and support: Professor David Clark (Glasgow), Dr Lizanne Henderson, Professor Sean Johnston, Dr Valentina Bold, Dr Sandy Whitelaw, Isabelle Clark, Dr Poshendra Satyal, Dr Lata Gautam, Lokendra P. Dhakal, Baikuntha P. Acharya, Deepak Raj Joshi, Anil Das, Venus and Ken Carew and Dr Ajay Singh.

My special thanks go to Dr Sandro Filho-Carnicelli with whom I share my office at UWS. He has painstakingly read most parts of my manuscript and suggested his valuable input to improve it. I also thank Steven Miles, who was studying for his doctorate together with me at the University of Glasgow Dumfries Campus, for his insight and the stimulating discussions on some of the arguments presented in this book. Another person who has meticulously gone through this manuscript several times is Mary MacIlwraith, who has been most helpful in her proofreading services to me, for which I am very much indebted.

The person who encouraged me to present my work in a book is Professor Alison Phipps from the University of Glasgow, who was the internal examiner for my doctoral thesis. While having lunch together after my successful viva she suggested I should publish my work. My thesis examiner Professor Peter Burns and the chairman of my thesis examination committee Dr David Borthwick (Glasgow) also encouraged me to publish and shared their opinion that it would make a valuable contribution to scholarship in Scottish studies, especially from a scholar who comes from a different socio-cultural background. I thank them all.

Finally, I thank my wife Taptika and son Nishad for their never-ending personal support and great patience.

Preface

My question in this book is: what role does tourism play in the imagining of the Scottish nation in contemporary Scotland? This question is informed by two important considerations: (i) that tourist sites are socio-cultural constructions and different tourism regions, spaces and sites may produce different narratives for tourists; (ii) that not all tourism sites or images and icons run a single discourse, as each touristic region or area is different from others in terms of the history it represents and the image and icons it is associated with. I was aware that many people believe the image of Scotland in tourism is unfairly tilted towards one region, the Scottish Highlands, and that this has resulted in a highly stereotyped identity of Scotland that favours this region. Thus, in this book I have chosen the relatively less known south-west and the central belt as my field.

The scope of this study is not confined to tourism attractions and heritage sites alone. It is also about historical accounts, cultural icons and images, events and celebrations and how they represent Scotland and create a meaning of the Scottish nation. To achieve my objective I have looked into different tourist attractions, icons, activities and accounts and treated each of these as a complete case or narrative and applied a full set of separate research tools for each case chosen. This gave me varied data that were primarily collected from field research using five main strategies: observation, interview, questionnaire survey, covert observation and field notes. I collected secondary data from various documentary sources that were identified in the course of this study. They were most widely consulted while interpreting the data in the later stages.

I would like to briefly explain how data were obtained. I relied widely on field observation so that I could capture the physical setting of different attractions and their atmosphere to draw inferences from them. In order to understand how the cultural icons, signs and markers of Scotland are presented to tourists, I undertook participant observation of different events, celebrations and activities. I conducted both structured and unstructured interviews with tourists and promoters of heritage and tourism events. Some of them said they preferred not to be interviewed and instead asked for questionnaire surveys to be filled in at their leisure. In addition, various forms of unobtrusive data, for example CD ROM, promotional brochures, websites, photos and images, museum artefacts, monuments and inscriptions were also consulted with a belief that we can learn about our society by investigating the material items produced within the culture: the texts and objects that groups of humans produce are embedded within the larger ideas those groups have, whether shared or contested.

The data obtained were selectively transcribed based on their nature, purpose and contribution to research. They were then coded, looking for themes to emerge which were later organised, and each emergent theme was presented as a separate chapter. I would also like to mention here that though they are not divided as such, the chapters here are organised in two parts. The first three chapters introduce the approach, lay the foundation for this study and are largely based on secondary materials. The following four chapters are based on empirical fieldwork carried out during 2008–2012. The final chapter is the conclusion. Each empirical chapter is organised as a standalone chapter and readers can comprehend the argument without reading the preceding or following chapters.

The materials in this book are based on my doctoral research. The topic was conceived slightly earlier during my MLitt programme in Tourism, Heritage and Development at the University of Glasgow. The first few weeks of the MLitt programme immersed me in Scottish history and culture and I realised that there was a deeper interaction of tourism with the Scottish nation as the touristic heritage of Scotland persistently represented its cultural identity, national image and distinctive characteristics. In the middle of my MLitt course I transferred to a PhD programme to pursue this area. However, it did not take long for me to realise that this was not a new area and that scholars have sporadically dealt with this in the past. This realisation was enough to make me concerned. Thus, I thought of sending my initial results for publication to test the validity of my claims and make sure that my analysis was original and was making a useful contribution to the field. At different stages the findings from the field were reported in the form of journal papers (Bhandari, 2008; 2010a; 2011; 2013). Thus, some of the material presented in this book has been published in the following forms: 'Touristification of cultural resources: A case study of Robert Burns', *TOURISM: An International Interdisciplinary Journal* 56 (3) (2008), 283–293; 'Burnishing nationalism: Touring Burns and authenticity in Scotland, *Tourism Culture and Communication'* 10 (2) (2010), 137–147; 'Recreating heritage in the southwest of Scotland', *Current Issues in Tourism* 14 (7) (2011), 669–683; 'Imagining the Scottish nation: Tourism and homeland nationalism in Scotland', *Current Issues in Tourism* (2013) (DOI: 10.1080/13683500.2013.789005) (www.tandfonline.com). I would like to thank the publishers for allowing me to use some of them in this book.

1 Introduction

Tourism is important in the ideological representation of a nation. By representing a particular or chosen narrative of a nation, tourism transmits a meaning of the nation. In many instances, this meaning has been orchestrated and exploited by regimes to present a desired narrative of the country by either political manipulation or through contrived construction of interpretation at touristic sites. In other cases, tourism narrates the 'national' story through the way various events or sites are socio-culturally constructed, arranged and interpreted to tourists. Either way, such acts help present a particular way of looking at the society that tourists travel to and tourism becomes interwoven with the meaning or ideology of the nation which at times produces a 'version' of its national identity and in a way articulates its 'nationhood': this book is about such a role of tourism in Scotland.

This book examines how tourism as a carrier of national icons and images exemplifies the idea of nationalism in Scotland. Aspects of 'nation' or 'nationhood' represented in tourism have received some attention from scholars of tourism, but they are focused more on how tourism brings changes to local identity, specifically to local communities or host cultures. The larger area that tourism can have an effect on, the 'national' community, has been dealt with by few scholars, who have largely argued that through tourism a country will seek to stress its own particular character and uniqueness and portray itself in a way that flatters and reinforces national identity. This work looks into the collective identity embedded in Scottish tourism to see how Scotland represents a 'national' sense to visitors.

I set out to see the contemporary story of Scottish tourism through the lens of historical resources and focused on Scottish heritage attractions at three levels: national, regional and personal. Lowenthal (1975) writes that through time certain heritage assumes a national importance that symbolises a society's shared recollections and represents national ideals. At the regional level, some familiar landmarks represent their collective past and can stir emotions and contribute to a local heritage experience. At the personal level, some heritage attractions draw people who possess emotional

Figure 1.1 Different levels of heritage within a national context

connections to a particular place. This is manifested by a search for historical roots and historical identity and an increased appreciation for one's culture and family legacy (Timothy & Boyd, 2003). In this book I am concerned with the narrative, either explicit or implicit, produced in the heritage-related tourism sites at each of these levels in Scotland. However, the boundaries between the three levels are not absolutely distinct and there can be an overlap between them, for example regional heritage can extend beyond the national, personal heritage can intersect and extend beyond regional heritage, and personal heritage can extend beyond national heritage (see Figure 1.1).

I look into how the three different levels of heritage intersect to produce stories of Scotland and how these stories interact with each other to produce the 'national' narrative through tourism. The heritage of the city of Edinburgh, Robert Burns and Robert the Bruce, for example, are some of the important 'national' icons this book looks into. Burns and Bruce also represent the important heritage of the south-west region where the empirical part of this book is primarily based. I explore how at a personal level genealogical heritage plays a part in articulating a sense of Scottish nationhood.

The city of Edinburgh is one of the most revered capital cities in Europe. Scholars have often described capital cities as an embodiment of their nations. For example, Baedeker (1900) writes of Paris, 'Paris is not only the political metropolis of France, but also the centre of artistic, scientific, commercial and industrial life of the nation' (cited in MacCannell, 1999: 48). Edinburgh is the premier tourist destination in Scotland and hosts historical and cultural attractions that are strongly embedded within the identity of the Scottish nation. One of the most popular ways visitors encounter the city of Edinburgh – its history, culture and archaeology – is through a sightseeing tour of the city on an open-top tour bus. I will elaborate on how the guides on the tour busses assert Scottish nationhood and distinctive national identity in the city of Edinburgh.

The other two Scottish icons, Robert Burns and Robert the Bruce, are national heroes of Scotland. Smith (1991) writes that a nation provides repertoires of shared values, symbols and traditions that enhance the bond between its members. One such repertoire is produced through national heroes who are celebrated, as this reminds members of the nation of their common heritage, identity and belonging. In Scotland, celebrations of Robert Burns and Robert the Bruce are not limited to specific times of the year, but they are marked each day at tourist sites and attractions. Besides, they are venerated by millions of people every day through various other tourism outlets, brochures and websites where their images and stories are presented to tourists. I argue that Burns and Bruce are value-laden icons and their touristification evokes the emotion of Scottish nationhood.

But the heritage of Bruce and Burns is also regional, as they have strong associations with the south-west region of Scotland. Examining the way authenticity is articulated through the regional heritage of Burns, I argue that the poet is effectively mobilised to produce a narrative that enhances the authentic Scottish nationhood. This happens through a variety of ways: for instance, the region is characterised by ruralness (Gillespie, 2011). Rurality has been associated with being real and authentic and this is characteristic of Burns' genre, as he is claimed to be the representative of the 'common man' in his writings. The presentation of Burns in tourism in this region matches the genre he represents: that is, to the tourists, Burns is presented in an authentic, rural and pastoral setting, mostly in the houses where he lived that have now been turned into museums. Scholars who have typified literary tourism argue that museums are the main destination of choice for literary tourists, as the dwellings are preserved and presented as original and authentic. While the touristic quest for authenticity is not new, the notion of authenticity at Burns museums has a close resonance with the ideals of nationalists, whose principal aim is to achieve authentic or ancient nationhood.

In contrast to Robert Burns, who has always belonged to this region, Robert the Bruce's legacy with this region in terms of tourism is largely sketchy. Historically, there has been enough of a story of Bruce's association with this region, but Bruce-related tourism was more or less restricted to being in and around Stirling, mainly at the Bannockburn war memorial. In the last 15 years, a trust dedicated to Bruce's legacy in the south-west region has taken the initiative to revive his historical association with this region. Bruce's heritage in this region has been recreated to develop sites as tourist attractions. This is not new, though. Heritage is 'about negotiation' – about using the past, and collective or individual memories, to negotiate new ways of being and expressing identity (Smith, 2006: 4, cited in Hodge & Baranek, 2011). But the effort to bring Bruce's heritage to the region is not neutral or value-free, as Bruce promoters are aware of the 'political' significance of bringing him to the region. Bruce is not alone in being recreated for tourists. There is also an event organised annually to celebrate this region's heritage, but much of the event is organised around Highland games, emphasising Highland culture. Recreating heritage in the region by introducing a more generic and homogenous heritage to this region helps tourism by providing a more identifiable image, but the fact I take note of, that both of these examples of heritage are inextricably linked to Scottish nationalism, cannot be ignored altogether.

I explore in detail how at a personal level genealogical heritage plays a part in articulating a sense of Scottish nationhood. Some scholars have ascribed the essence of the Scottish tourism brand to being founded deeply on its sense of history. One of the iconic marks in the history of Scotland is the Clearances in the Scottish Highlands (Prebble, 1982), and the consequent outcome of this time was Scottish emigration. Emigration from Scotland did not remain confined to the Highlands but was the trend across Scotland. The south-west region witnessed a considerable outward migration and the volume of emigration from Dumfries was markedly high (Brock, 1999: 163; also see Murdoch, 2010). The significance of this emigration today is that there is a large population of Scottish diaspora, for whom Scotland forms part of their personal heritage. I try to explain the way diasporas' visits to their native land connect with the notion of 'homeland' nationalism. I depart from the fundamental approach that tourism is the 'industry of difference' and argue, on the contrary, that genealogical tourism is driven by the search for affinity and commonness: rather than travelling away from home, these tourists are travelling to their native 'home'. I argue that the 'commonness' with their 'native' land reinforces the sense of affinity that resonates closely with the ideals of 'nationalists'. Besides, genealogy has another dimension in the study of nationalism, which some scholars have viewed through two strands – ethnic and civic. The preference for bringing in Scottish-descendant tourists, additionally, also sheds light on the ethnic dimension of Scottish nationalism.

Overall, this book sheds light on the hitherto understudied aspects of the 'nation' and 'nationalism' represented in tourism. The issue has become highly topical as Scotland is on the verge of defining its identity one more time. At the time of writing, Scottish national politics is dominated by debate on the opportunities and consequences of independence: the proposed Scottish independence referendum is less than a year away. This book is informed by the contemporary political debate in Scotland and builds on earlier studies that have linked heritage, tourism and nationalism; and reasserts that 'nation' and 'nationalism' are ideologically enshrined in the concept of tourism. It shows how tourism can act as a means to express and represent 'nation' and 'nationalism' in various forms and narratives.

Tourism and National Identity

The nature of tourism that represents 'us' to 'them' gives rise to the possibility that presenting a destination as 'the other' is essentially the way that asserts the 'national' identity of the nation, because in doing so it helps in self-identification. The 'process of self-definition and location is in many ways the key to national identity', writes Smith (1991: 17). There is a growing interest in the way tourism interacts with national identity while creating a distinctive national character of the destination. Many scholars look into tourism through the lens of heritage and the way it helps shape national identity and nationalism (Cheung, 1999; Cohen, 2010; Henderson, 2001; Light, 2001; Morgan & Pritchard, 1998; Palmer, 1999; Pretes, 2003; Pritchard & Morgan, 2001; Tnsescu, 2006). They take the view that national identity and nation are complex constructs composed of a number of interrelated components: ethnic, cultural, territorial, economic, legal and political.

The use of many symbols, uniforms, ceremonies and monuments is an important method through which members of a nation are reminded of their heritage and cultural kinship. It is an important way in which the nation is narrated to its members. French sociologist Lanfant acknowledges the role of heritage tourism in shaping identity and depicting 'nationness' through a similar narration. She writes, 'imperceptibly the place becomes determined by external forces and reconstructed from a touristic point of view' (1995a: 5). The system of the promotion of tourism indirectly intervenes in cultural references, in the definition of the values, signs, supports and markers of identity (1995a: 8) and can greatly define and dictate the positioning of identity and foster a sense of distinctiveness under various circumstances and dispositions.

There has been increased interest in looking into the role of tourism in articulating national identity in recent years (Frew & White, 2011; Lepp & Haris, 2008; Park, 2010; Pretes, 2003; Pitchford, 1995, 2006; Shaffer, 2001). For example, in the American context, Shaffer (2001) describes how domestic tourism in the US, beginning in the late 1800s, was an integral component in the process of national identity formation. Citizen tourists forged common understandings of what it was to be an American through the consumption of patriotic landmarks, grandiose landscapes and the experience of moving westward. I have shown elsewhere that tourism image is closely bound up with the country's culture and its national identity, and any change in the country's national identity can demand a corresponding adjustment in the country's tourism image (Bhandari, 2010b). I argue that the dictatorial Nepalese monarchy effectively employed tourism to bolster its image and construct a 'contrived' national identity to pursue aggressive nationalism on which the monarchy thrived politically.

In their edited volume *Tourism and National Identities*, Frew and White (2011) demonstrate that national identity and tourism intersect, overlap and traverse; and that this presents an opportunity for authorities to capture the imagination of tourists by referring to various aspects of national identity. They argue that gaining a better understanding of national identity is itself a worthwhile endeavour, and integrating this with links to tourism adds to its significance. The connection between tourism and national identity is apparent via the promotional activities of tourism authorities in relation to cultural activities, events and heritage. They recognise a need to better understand the multifaceted and complex connections between people and places, and argue for the development of national identity-related products.

However, developing national identity-related products is a difficult proposition as this can create contention within the country. There can also be debate on how such products should be packaged to tourists because they can be counter-productive: not all types of visitors may feel comfortable with the nature of such 'national' products. One important characteristic of national identity is that it is also a negative force and in many cases a source of aggression. According to Hobsbawm (1999: 169), nationalism by definition excludes 'all who do not belong to its own nation, that is, the vast majority of the human race'. Thus, deliberately having products that boast of national pride can be highly political in nature. The 'nationalistic' sentiment present in those tourism products can create uneasiness in some types of visitors, especially if they are not part of that heritage or if they are from a former imperialist power.

Thus, the desirability of tourism products designed to exalt national pride can be debated, but developing heritage to tell the nationalist story can potentially help in building national identity, argues Pitchford (2008). In the same tone, Park (2010) argues that heritage tourism experiences are indicative of cultural primordials, which emphasise ethnic or racial origins and indicate innate cultural manifestations of the nation. She concludes that domestic heritage tourism is not just an act of the touristic consumption of heritage artefacts but also a reaffirmation of national meanings and values. There are certain attributes of nation that constantly give people a sense of oneness. It is a pride, a sentiment, a character that arguably make a people a nation, that endow them with a national identity, and these are the ideals embodied in the national symbols, ceremonies and customs of a nation (Palmer, 1999) – which are very much present in tourism.

There are numerous studies which have shown the 'nationalist' role played by tourism. Edensor (1998) has shown that the touristic narrative produced at the Taj Mahal in India varies to a great extent. For some the Taj is an evocative symbol of the colonial past, for others it is a symbolic centre of Islamic power and for many of the thousands of tourists who visit it each year it is simply a monument of love. Most importantly, he believes that at the Taj Mahal Indian nationhood is articulated and performed. Pitchford (2006) has shown that tourists who visit Wales are exposed to almost every piece of the national story in some form: museums and other attractions that focus on a group's history and culture serve as a medium to project ethnic and nationalist messages and help to build a revalued collective identity. In another study of Wales, Prichard and Morgan (2001) argue that the influence of repressive and liberating historical, political and cultural discourses is importantly enshrined in tourism representations.

Scholars have made strong reference to the role of tourism and the 'national' manifestation of Scotland. Most potently, the historian Hugh Trevor-Roper (1983) recounts this role through three aspects of the Highland tradition of Scotland which form an intrinsic part of Scottish national identity. The first of these is the invention of a Scots-Gaelic epic poet called Ossian whose supposed writing was 'discovered' and 'translated' in the 1760s. Promoters of Ossian, Trevor-Roper contends, popularised the idea that Scottish-Highland culture was a distinct and ancient one. The second is the invention of the modern kilt sometime after 1727 by a Quaker industrialist named Thomas Rawlinson and its quick adoption in many parts of the Highlands and Northern Lowlands by about 1768. The third invented aspect of the Highland tradition of Scotland, Trevor-Roper argues, is that of tartan. Family tartans, as they are now generally conceived, probably never existed. Instead, tartans probably were regionally based with different patterns belonging to different areas of the country. What tartan one wore was mainly a decision based on preference or fashion.

According to Trevor-Roper (1983), the wearing of the kilt and tartan became popular in the 19th century because of the romantic interest in the idea of the noble savage and the exploits of the Highland regiments in India and America. Thus, following the lifting of the ban on Highland dress that was imposed after the 1745 Jacobite Rebellion, Highland noblemen, anglicised Scottish peers, improving gentry, well-educated Edinburgh lawyers and prudent merchants of Aberdeen – 'men who were not constrained by poverty and who would never have to skip over rocks and bogs or lie all night in the hills' – took to wearing the modern kilt as a new fashion. In this way, the entire Scottish nation adopted the bogus Highland symbols of kilt and tartan.

In her book *Tourism and Identity in Scotland*, Grenier (2005) again traces history to examine the role of tourism in asserting a distinctive Scottish identity. She looks into the various contributing factors in the development of Scottish tourism that left a significant mark on the shaping of its tourism identity. She draws a closer analogy between the growth of Highland sporting activity and British nationalism, as sports required the same sort of abilities as warfare. She says that promoters of tourism use history by presenting it as a loose collection of incidents with little sense of a unifying thread to emphasise Scottish differentness and downplay any threat posed by its independent past. According to Grenier, Scotland's political nationalism assumed greater relevance after the late 19th and 20th centuries, when the state became more centralised with the expansion of politics to a greater percentage of citizens and in more and more areas of society. She maintains that tourism played a central, but deprecating, part in British understanding of Scotland and 'triviality of the vision of Scotland's past produced by tourism had significant consequences for the development of the country's national identity' (2005: 156). Grenier also believes that tourism representations in Scotland were highly selective and because of this representativeness of only part of the country they became symbols of the whole (2005: 159), pointing to the predominance of Highland iconography in Scottish tourism. What Grenier suggests is that the Scottish Highlands and Lowlands are separate entities and there is a dichotomy between them about which some authors, such as MacDonald (1997), do not really agree.

In fact, MacDonald (1997), in her anthropological study of Gaelic identity, suggests that the Highland/Lowland dichotomy is a myth created by the English. She examines how the Gaelic renaissance in Scotland is helping in '(re)imagining community' through the appropriation and incorporation of Gaelic culture and distinctiveness into Scottish national identity. The revival of Gaelic, she concludes, has elevated it to be one of the most important aspects of identity amongst a much wider range of ways of identifying. This revivalism has further ramifications for Scottish nationalism – both romantic and political. Now, increasingly, Gaelic is being cast as the language of Scotland, not confined within the Highlands. Indeed, in order to enhance Scotland's distinctiveness vis-à-vis England, Gaelic is now 'increasingly being used in the touristic marketing of Scotland as a whole' (1997: 240).

In their influential study, sociologists McCrone *et al.* (1995) have looked into the rise of heritage and its corresponding connotations for Scotland. They believe that nationalism is emerging as a device for bolstering a nation-state's fading popularity and a means for imagining a form of political community. They examine how three different premier agencies responsible for heritage in Scotland view it, and find that heritage is seen by each of the three agencies as 'product', 'artefacts' and 'conservative nationalism', respectively. Importantly, they construe that growth in political nationalism is less connected with the developing sense of cultural nationalism; instead they cautiously distance it from being a form of political nationalism.

McCrone *et al.* (1995) view the rise of cultural nationalism in the form of heritage as the analogue of political nationalism. They are careful not to accept the strong overlap between cultural and political nationalism. For example, they acknowledge that the political and cultural realm in Scotland is very much connected – which suggests that they are indirectly implying that cultural assertion is not free from political overtones. Second, their study is based on the premise that heritage is an important marker and manifestation of identity, which is to say implicitly that it is a form of nationalism: after all, Scottish nationalism, as is widely accepted, is about asserting their identity and distinctiveness. However, they acknowledge that the revival of both cultural and political nationalism in Scotland is plausibly expressed through heritage, which is inextricably linked to tourism.

Many studies of the role of tourism in the articulation of Scottish nationhood point out the role of the 'invented' markers and their dominance in representing Scotland. In contrast, studies of tourism and national identity elsewhere have been built on Anderson's (1991) notion of the 'imagined community', arguing that citizens conceptualise the nation through common shared experiences that help bring about a sense of community despite members not actually being able to know each other. For example, Pretes (2003) argues that tourism sights, such as censuses, maps and museums, may contain a discourse of nationalism. They may function in the same way as museums, guarding national heritage and history and preserving them for public display and allowing hegemonic cultural producers to project their values of national identity. Pretes believes such sights transmit the messages of the creators of the sites and encode a shaping of a common national identity, ultimately helping to construct an imagined community. This is because the idea of community is in one's mind and, as a mental construct, it condenses symbolically (Cohen, 1985a). In this process, tourism plays a part in manifesting and sometimes 'constructing' a shared national identity.

Many such studies do suggest a closer link between heritage and nationalism. Scholars have argued the role of tourism in the 'national' manifestation of Scotland has been mostly in a cultural rather than a strict political sense. Historical accounts further suggest that Scottish tourism developed largely through non-state actors, and the production of a particular narrative of Scotland was independent of any direct state-intervention. Amidst the existing body of knowledge on the interaction between tourism and nationalism in Scotland, this book stands out in two important ways. It presents the viewpoint of a researcher who is non-native, non-western and does not bring postmodern or post-colonial positions to the subject. Second, it studies the case of Scotland in the context of a territory that has largely been left untouched – the central belt and the south-west. We shall see these two areas in more detail.

The Location of the Author in the Study

The presence of the author in his own work has been debated since the publication of Barthes' 'Death of the Author' in 1968, in which he challenges the traditional, humanist concept of a single source of all meaning. Defying the concept of intentionality, i.e. a text meant literally what its author intended it to mean, Barthes (1977) launched an assault on the notion of human agency by highlighting the socially determined structure rather than the intentional acts of individuals. This argument was subsequently challenged by Foucault in 1969, who believed that the author cannot disappear that simply, because the author, or what Foucault terms 'author-function', is historically determined and culturally specific and whose effects persist (Foucault, 1980). However, Barthes' bold formulation can also be read as part of a general move towards reader-based studies of text, which mean that the author is no longer the source of all meaning, but one of the processes of interpreting the text: this is what I have done in this book. I have tried to read the various images, icons and narratives represented in Scottish tourism imagery and presented that imagery as I see them. However, agreeing with what Foucault has said, I believe my reading of them is not uninformed by my own historical and cultural background.

In social science research this debate on the location of the author has continued unabated. Denzin and Lincoln (2005) write that three interconnected generic activities define qualitative research. They go by a variety of different labels, including theory, analysis, ontology, epistemology and methodology. Behind these terms stand the personal biography of the researcher, who speaks from a particular class, gender, racial, cultural and ethnic community perspective. In other words, Denzin and Lincoln (2005) suggest that every researcher speaks from within a distinct interpretive community that is configured in its special way. In this context, it is imperative that I explain an important background that has shaped this study, that is, my own background and the reason for this book. I am male and from Nepal, a country that has no colonial relation with the United Kingdom and is still largely a traditional agrarian society. There is a deep affinity between Nepal and the

UK because Nepal contributes significantly to the UK's armed forces by supplying the Gurkha soldiers who are recruited from the country. In Nepal, the UK is understood as a unitary entity, and the existence of other 'national' units within the UK is largely unknown. As has been said, a qualitative researcher conducts 'a reading' to discover meaning embedded within text and brings his or her subjective experience to a text (Neuman, 2003: 76). The interpretation in this book is read through the author's perspective, which is informed by my background as a Nepali national and my perception of the UK until coming to Scotland for my post-graduate studies.

On many occasions positivists have challenged such an approach as lacking reliability or validity. However, an important tenet of interpretivism is that research cannot be understood as separate from the researcher. Tribe (2006) has argued that there are five factors at work in the knowledge force-field, i.e. *rules, ends, ideology, person* and *position*. According to Tribe, *rules* in knowledge-creation consist of those conventions that researchers subscribe to and work within, for example, discipline, paradigms and methodology. *Ends* refer to the purpose of knowledge, which is grounded in the belief that the pursuit of knowledge is never interest-free. *Ideology* is the common set of beliefs that guides thought and action. In my case, person and position are the most important to note. *Person* is identified as a substantive power in the knowledge force-fields, what Swain (2004: 102) calls 'the corporal selves of researchers ... as primary factors in the research process'. Hall (2004: 148) notes that, 'in terms of why we research what we do, one also cannot ignore the personal'. This point must be illustrated in my case.

My decision to pursue doctoral study in tourism was informed by previous work experience at the Nepalese Tourism Board. However, it is interesting to note why I chose the south-west of Scotland in relating tourism with nationalism. I come from that part of Nepal which is not strongly connected with the popular tourism areas of the country. The region does not fit within the stereotypical image of Nepal and is considered largely neglected in terms of tourism development. This correlates strongly to the south-west region of Scotland. Importantly, in the last few years there has been an increased debate for regionalism in Nepal which is gradually developing as a nationalistic movement in different manifestations. The choice of my study was largely informed by my own home experience. But the choice of Scotland was rather based on financial and personal considerations. I was not keen to undertake study which required a large amount of financial resources. I chose Scotland also because both tourism and nationalism are vibrant in there and I had this belief that the best supervision that could be gained in Scotland would be that concerned with Scotland. *Position*, according to Tribe (2006), describes the location of the researcher both in terms of geographical situatedness and positioning within a university department as well as location within an academic community and a wider language and cultural community. In terms of academic orientation, my previous post-graduate qualification in sociology has greatly shaped this study. However, this work was conducted whilst based in the School of Interdisciplinary Studies of the University of Glasgow and I was constantly interacting with scholars whose disciplinary backgrounds were varied. These facts have also influenced my approach to some extent.

The geographical situatedness has another dimension. This book is largely based on field study predominantly in the south-west region of Scotland. Qualitative researchers realise the cultural meaning of the social sciences by their reflection and by their sensibility (Mills, 1970: 14, cited in Holliday, 2007: 20). I lived in Dumfries, a small town in the study region, during the entire study period, which has positive and negative aspects, as follows: living in Dumfries, I was able to participate in various tourism activities in the region, interact with local people, and look into things from a local perspective, which helped me bring my own subjective experience of the field to this research. In essence, this made the whole of this research a form of participant observation, as it has been noted, '... in a sense all social research is a form of participant observation' (Atkinson & Hammersley, 1994, cited in Holliday, 2007: 17). Conversely, living in Dumfries also means that the interpretation and readings of the data are strongly informed by a regional perspective of Dumfries and the people from this region.

Tourism in South-West Scotland

Geographically, this work is based on field research in the central belt and the south-west of Scotland – mainly the Dumfries and Galloway region. Popularly these regions fall within the Scottish Lowland territory. Reasons for the selection of the south-west of Scotland for this research are as follows. Earlier scholars have argued that Highland tourism embodies Highlandism, which exemplifies Scottish nationalism. Compared to the Scottish Highlands, where there is no dearth of studies in tourism, the region of the south-west is less studied in terms of its heritage and touristic identity. The region has its own identity that is distinct from the Highlands, suggesting it bears less proximity to the popular imagery of Scotland. Throughout history the south-west has remained isolated and maintained a relative autonomy. It is a borderland area, where Scotland and England meet, and is that part of Scotland relatively isolated from the rest of the country, poorly served by road, and still linked insufficiently by rail to Edinburgh and

Glasgow (Gillespie, 2011; Lynch, 2005). The region does not contain any airports, although Prestwick (near Ayr), Glasgow and Edinburgh are accessible within two hours (Gillespie, 2011).

The predominant area of the south-west falls into the administrative region of Dumfries and Galloway. The Galloway Project (1968) identifies the most distinctive feature of this part of Scotland as being its consistent remoteness throughout history, despite its geographical proximity to population centres. However, this remoteness was also corrected to some extent by the greater sea links this region enjoyed. According to the project report, this remoteness, born of an internal desire for independence and an external lack of interest in a narrow resource base, is even acknowledged in the very name given to the area some 800 years ago. Galloway means 'land of strangers' in Gaelic and the perpetuation of this separatist image is documented elsewhere (The Galloway Project, 1968). As a border region, it has an intricate and sustained regional identity constructed out of an undisturbed sense of place, particularly true of a community which is culturally bounded and relatively isolated from other regions and influences (Lynch, 2005).

Tourism is fundamental to the Dumfries and Galloway economy. The most recent Scottish Tourism Economic Activity Monitor report has concluded that, in 2009, approximately 5977 jobs (full-time equivalents) were supported by direct tourist expenditure in the region, and a further 1358 jobs were supported by indirect revenue from tourism (Dumfries & Galloway Regional Tourism Strategy 2011–2016, undated). It is estimated that tourism accounted for 11% of employment in Dumfries and Galloway – placing it in the top three of employment sectors.

However, it remains one of the least visited regions of Scotland, along with Angus, Fife and the neighbouring Scottish Borders (Gillespie, 2011). According to VisitScotland (2011), visitors made 15.71 million trips to Scotland and spent £4508 million in 2011. The share of the Dumfries and Galloway region was 0.869 million trips and £193 million, which represents 5.53% and 4.28% respectively. The main purposes of visiting the region are: holiday (domestic 79%; overseas 56%), visiting friends and relatives (domestic 13%; overseas 27%) and business (domestic 8%; overseas 16%). The low figure for business visitors is to be expected in the region because it is rural and there are very limited business activities there. April–September is the most visited time of the year, receiving 74% of the total visitors (VisitScotland, 2011). The visitor pattern is dominated by short-stay trips of one–three nights, which account for almost 55% of the total visits to the region. But, comparatively, this is better than the overall percentage in Scotland, which receives 67% of visitors staying for one–three days. The average UK tourist trip in the region is 3.7 days, which is also better than the national average of 3.4 days. But the average trip for overseas tourists is poor (6.4 days) in comparison to the national average (7.5 days).

In order to improve the region's poor performance in tourism, the industry has developed the Dumfries and Galloway Regional Tourism Strategy 2011–2016 to strengthen tourism in the region. The strategy is aimed at fostering joint partnerships between organisations working in the tourism industry, namely, Dumfries and Galloway Council, Destination Dumfries & Galloway, and VisitScotland. The development of the new Regional Tourism Strategy has brought all of the key partners together to develop a strategy that supports all concerned with the tourism industry in Dumfries and Galloway. The objective is to achieve Scotland's 'national' tourism ambition – which is to grow the value of Scottish tourism by 50% between 2006 and 2015, equal to a consistent annual growth rate of 4%. This challenge is set against a global forecast of 4–5% growth until the year 2020 by the World Trade Organisation. According to the Dumfries and Galloway Regional Tourism Strategy 2011–2016, the value of tourism to the region in 2006 was £226 million and in 2009 this rose to £269 million, an increase of 19%. The ambition is to achieve an annual worth of £340 million into the local economy by 2015 (Dumfries & Galloway Regional Tourism Strategy 2011–2016, undated).

Tourism in the region is diversified. The regional website of VisitScotland says, 'Visit mysterious castles and fascinating museums one day and enjoy mountain biking through forests the next. Dumfries and Galloway has so much to offer from art galleries, nature reserves and glorious gardens to Scotland's only Food Town in Castle Douglas.' The region is associated with some of the iconic heritages in Scotland, for example the heritage of Robert Burns, Robert the Bruce and the World Famous Old Blacksmiths Shop in Gretna Green, to note a few. The World Famous Old Blacksmiths Shop in Gretna Green, which received three-quarters of a million tourists in 2012, is Scotland's seventh most visited free attraction (VisitScotland, 2013c). Despite its strong association with 'national' heroes like Robert Burns and Robert the Bruce, attractions associated with these figures are not encouraging and are rated far below other attractions. Other main attractions in the region are activity centres like the Mabie Forest (135,000 visitors), Dalbeattie Forest (105,000 visitors), Mabie Farm Park (73,913 visitors) and Cream O' Galloway (65,900 visitors) (VisitScotland, 2011). Interestingly, Burns' House, which is the star attraction in Dumfries, receives only slightly more than 15,000 visitors annually (VisitScotland, 2010).

One of the recent efforts to attract tourists to the region has been through the development of theme towns. Three small towns, namely,

Wigtown, Kirkudbright and Castle Douglas, have been branded as distinct theme towns, based on books, artists and food, respectively – in an attempt to make them more attractive to visitors and thereby improve their economy. Macleod (2009), who has examined whether the new identities possessed by the towns have enhanced their development, finds that branding as theme towns has helped them develop in terms of their economy and culture. More importantly, according to him, the branding effort has enhanced their social capital, which has been underappreciated by planners and observers.

The three theme towns have established a new initiative known as Glorious Galloway to promote them, using the strap line 'Glorious Galloway It's Absolutely F.A.B. (Food-Arts-Books) and SO much more'. A website and a brochure have been produced which colourfully illustrate the towns and the region, as well as advertising businesses based in the towns. Macleod notes that in marketing terms, the development of a 'cluster' of attractions will help create a stronger pull for visitors.

Institutionally, there has been a larger private-sector-led initiative to promote tourism in the region in recent years. For example, Destination Dumfries and Galloway is a commercially driven, private-sector-led partnership that aims to continually improve tourism in ways that benefit local businesses, communities and visitors. They ensure that Dumfries and Galloway offers a high quality visitor experience, and work in close partnership with public agencies and community and business groups in order to achieve this. Their projects include: seasonal marketing campaigns to promote the area; essential market research; a regional consumer website; an industry-facing website; and a range of informative workshops and networking events for local businesses.

In the next chapter we will see the historicity of interaction between tourism and nationalism in Scotland. Chapter 3 discusses the touristic production of Scotland through the framing of identity and shows how a distinctive image of Scotland has been reinforced for almost two centuries by a peculiar combination of geography, emigration, social stratification, romantic appeal and attachment to literature and art. Chapters 4–7 are empirical chapters based on the author's fieldwork in the central belt and the southwest of Scotland. Chapter 4 draws on the role of tour guides as 'mediators' of local culture to show how they exemplify the idea of the Scottish nation and nationhood during their tours on the Edinburgh tour buses. Chapter 5 looks into the cases of the regional heritage of Robert the Bruce and the Border Gathering event and illustrates how dominant heritage is directed towards forming a uniform and homogenous identity. Chapter 6 examines Robert Burns' cult status and looks into the notion of authenticity in his heritage that plays a semiotic role in presenting a symbolic version of Scottish national identity. Chapter 7 explores how the personal enrichment of visiting one's 'ancient' nation can reinforce the common cultural affinity of tourists to their ancestral land. Chapter 8 presents a summative discussion of earlier chapters and the meaning we can draw from them.

2 Tourism and Nationalism in Scotland

Tourism has played a significant role in the evolution of the 'viewing of Scotland' (Hughes, 1992). This viewing of Scotland has happened through the reading of the culture, icons and images of the Scottish nation presented to visitors, which started long before the advent of modern tourism. 'Literary medievalism', according to Smith (1991), in the 18th century played a major part in the reconstruction of a community's history and culture. The movement of 'literary medievalism' was so much of an influence that intellectuals from each emergent nation started to 'rediscover' and 'review' it as objectification of the underlying values and culture of each nation, which strengthened the emerging consciousness of each nation's ethnic background and hence its ethnic nationalism (Smith, 1991: 88–89). Interestingly, this started in Scotland with the cult of the Ossian poems. The Ossian phenomenon was one of the first instances of 'literary tourism', bringing tourists to places apparently mentioned by Ossian, and seemingly touched by the magic associated with his mystical vision of the Celtic past (Squire, 1994, cited in Inglis & Holmes, 2003).

The foundation of modern tourism in Scotland began in the aftermath of the unsuccessful attempt in 1745 to establish a Stuart monarchy in Great Britain. That incident, on one hand, increased travellers' interest in its culture and society and, on the other hand, it also unfolded an era of multiple socio-economic and political developments in the history of the Scottish nation (Durie, 2003; Gold & Gold, 1995). The 1745 'uprising' quickened the absorption of Scotland into the new British state and opened up opportunities for travellers and tourists to visit in ever increasing numbers. It is after this incident that the construction of physical infrastructures like roads, bridges and renovation of buildings and forts was started in Scotland, mostly for military purposes, which helped set up tourism activities. The uprising also created an interest in the Scottish Highlands and travellers started visiting the area: this was instrumental in creating an early impression of Scotland.

Scotland is a 'touristified' nation in the sense that its 'nationness' is highly exploited by tourism and vice versa. Grenier (2006: 1000) writes, 'the industry of tourism and the idea of Scotland developed alongside each other; Scotland played a disproportionately important role in the history of tourism, and tourism a disproportionately important role in the history of modern Scotland'. After 1790, when tourism expansion accelerated with the development of transportation technology, tourism in great measure contributed to the creation of the idea of Scotland, in which some events and actors were particularly noteworthy, for example, the role of Sir Walter Scott and royal visitors.

Sir Walter Scott played a very important role in the early promotion of Scotland, which led to the creation of what some scholars call 'Highlandism' (Grenier, 2006: 1003). Scott's poems and novels featured Scotland as a 'Romantic' country, which was important from the point of view of tourism, as it offered a unique and distinctive image of Scotland, and showed that it was different from England. Additionally, Scott played an eminent role in demystifying the Highlands by appropriating Highland culture when George IV visited Edinburgh in 1822. Together with Sir Walter Scott's novels, the increasing passion for the Romantic movement witnessed all over Western Europe in the 19th century encouraged an enthusiastic promotion of the Scottish landscape and exotic mountains: thus the iconography of the Scottish natural and cultural landscape received an even greater endorsement. Romanticism fuelled an antiquarianism and scholarly interest in Medievalism, viewing the landscape in terms of heroic figures involved in epic events and displaying flawless chivalry despite the barbarity of the times in which they lived (Gold & Gold, 1995: 62). Scotland's untouched nature and unexplored landscape drew huge interest from tourists.

The role of Queen Victoria in the development of tourism in Scotland is noteworthy (Durie, 2003; Gold & Gold, 1995; Long & Palmer, 2007). After the royal visit of 1822, it was the acquisition of Balmoral in the Dee Valley in 1848 by Prince Albert that made the biggest contribution to Scottish tourism. The subsequent royal visits to Balmoral inspired people to visit Highland estates, taking part in sporting activity. Queen Victoria published her journal on her life in Balmoral, giving extra impetus to people's desire to travel north of the border. Palmer (2007) admits that with respect to British identity, the monarchy, as a tourism representation tool, supports the modernist approach to nationality. The modernist approach believes that nations are products of industrialisation and that the political and national units of a nation should be congruent. British royalty was used, in this sense, as a tool to represent a uniform British identity across Great Britain, which is not unnatural, given the halcyon days of Unionist nationalism. However, I will argue later that Unionist nationalism, in the case of Scotland, did not intend to dissolve Scottish identity into that of its English neighbour, but it did appreciate Scottish distinctiveness.

Tourism not only created a distinctive image of Scotland to outside visitors, it was also important for Scots themselves. McCrone (2001) believes that the consequence of the Union of Parliament of 1707 was that Scotland's cultural distinctiveness vis-à-vis England appeared thin. Davidson (2000) believes that this was also partly because, despite Scotland being a separate country before the Union, the country lacked a cohesive image for people to identify with. The advent of tourism that started as an exploratory visit by travellers in search of a 'dreadful country', as some of them termed it, slowly graduated towards major economic activity, and provided a foundation for Scottish people to develop a distinct centrifugal identity. On the one hand, the improvements in logistics by a simplified postal and financial network and subsequent travel accounts helped ignorance and prejudice about Scotland to fade in northern Britain as Scotland slowly started to draw visitors' interest (Durie, 2003: 35). On the other hand, with the discovery of the kilt, which was a much later invention (Trevor-Roper, 1983), tourism helped to create a distinctive Scottish identity.

It can be argued that the role of tourism in the formation and manifestation of Scottish identity was dominant, but whether that was an appropriate identity is a highly debatable issue. There is no unanimity between scholars on this. Some commentators have shown that tourism played an enormous role in the shaping of Scottish national identity. Trevor-Roper (1983: 16) has attempted to show, in his *Invention of Tradition* thesis, that the creation of an independent Highland tradition, and the imposition of new tradition, with its outward badges, on the whole Scottish nation, was the work of the 18th and early 19th century, and tourism played a considerable part in creating this identity. Many scholars do not accept his point however (see Ascherson, 2010; Cheape, 1995). In his book on tartan, Cheape (1995) demonstrates that it is not a late invention. Furthermore, Trevor-Roper's views on the kilt as a modern phenomenon fail to give us an answer to the question: if the kilt had not been of great relevance as a symbol for Scottish national identity long before why did it seem necessary to ban it as a true element of Highland life after the rebellion of 1745?

But adoption of 'false Highland traditions' (Devine, 1994: 86) in the subsequent years was meaningful in forming 'the symbolic basis of a new Scottish identity'. An incident that was remarkable in this was the royal visit to Scotland in the 19th century. Zuelow (2006) argues that the tourist impression during George IV's visit to Scotland in 1822 helped shape a new Scottish national memory and identity. He contends that the events of the 14 days of the visit made a tremendous contribution to the dialogue about the nature of Scottishness to the people who travelled to Edinburgh to witness the visit. However, some scholars see the role of tourism in Scotland as directed towards denigrating the identity and authenticity of Scotland. Grenier (2005: 159), for example, suggests that tourism played a central, but deprecating, part and was 'complicit in the "Balmoralization" of Scotland', as, according to her, practices which were of dubious historical authenticity and representative of only part of the country became symbols of the whole.

Similarly, Nairn (1981) is critical of the romanticism of popular culture that revolves around the images of tartan and bagpipes, which for him is a forgery. But this type of forgery is not new in tourism. There is always a gap between the touristic images and the social reality of any destination, which happens as a result of 'staged authenticity' (MacCannell, 1999). The staging as such 'is of crucial importance in the formation of tourists' impressions of a destination' (Cohen, 1993: 63). McCrone *et al.* (1995: 207) believe assertion of identity itself to be the main ingredient of identity: thus, the representation of Scotland made in tourism discourse, irrespective of its appropriateness, was meaningful to visitors. Whether or not tartanry or the images of the Highlands that tourism appropriated were a true representation of Scotland, they created a great cultural distinction and still assume enormous relevance as potent signifiers of Scottishness to most visitors (Butler, 1998).

Today, Scottish tourism is stocked with the iconography of Scottish identity and the emblem of Scottish nationhood. The images of tartan, whisky, bagpipes, Culloden, Bannockburn, Edinburgh Castle, Robert Burns, Sir Walter Scott, Robert the Bruce and so on are the prominent features in Scotland's tourism map. Many of these icons are strongly linked with the image of the Scottish nation and flatter its national identity. 'To boast about the resources of the country means to praise the idea of the nation', considers Lanfant (1995b: 33). Scholars have shown that some of these icons closely resonate with the ideals of nationalism and tourism which have produced a nationalist discourse at some heritage sites (see Aitchison, 1999; Edensor, 1997a; McCrone *et al.*, 1995). The role of tourism in the Scottish national consciousness is acknowledged by Davidson (2000: 134), who writes:

> Staging for the tourist in fact contributes to the invention of national cultures, or more precisely, the formation of national consciousness. Tourism is not simply a question of identity – in the sense of how Scotland was represented to non-Scots – rather than one of the consciousness of its habitants, but the process of constructing an image of

> Scotland for external consumption also contributed to the construction of an internal sense of what it meant to be Scottish.

Davidson's views indicate the cultural role played by tourism in Scotland. Given the ubiquitous presence of tourism this has extra significance. Tourism is absolutely vital to Scotland (MacLellan & Smith, 1998). It provides 13% of the total employment in Scotland. Tourism is spread across the country and all of the 14 Scottish tourist regions rely considerably on it. According to the latest available data, Scotland has a total of 682 listed tourist attractions; out of which 381 are chargeable and 301 are free attractions (VisitScotland, 2010). Heritage provides the main resource for tourist attractions. The most popular tourism activities undertaken include general sightseeing, exploring Scottish scenery, visiting castles and historic houses, museums, art galleries and heritage centres.

Heritage-related tourism attractions constitute the largest segment of attractions in Scotland. For example, castles and forts (58), museums and art galleries (225), heritage and visitor centres (100), historic houses and palaces (49), historic monuments and archaeological sites (30) and other historic properties (15) combined comprise 477 attractions, which account for 70% of total attractions (VisitScotland, 2010). Additionally, attractions that are categorised as natural reserves and wildlife; steam and heritage railways; industrial and craft works places also involve attractions that have close historical importance. In 2012, more than 1.89 million tourists visited its top free attraction, the National Museum of Scotland, and 1.23 million visited Edinburgh Castle, which is the top paid attraction – both of them being heritage based (VisitScotland, 2013c).

The main feature of heritage attractions in tourism is that they can act as places to showcase the nation's distinctiveness, its cultural richness and authenticity. As heritage by its very nature is steeped in the past, heritage tourism has been regarded as one of the mechanisms of dissemination for nationalism and other ideologically loaded discourses (Graham *et al.*, 2000). Tourism at heritage sites 'indirectly intervenes in cultural references, in the definition of the values, signs, supports and markers of identity' (Lanfant, 1995a: 8), and becomes the statement of the collective identity. Pitchford (2008) has labelled this type of tourism which relies on attractions in which collective identities are represented, interpreted and potentially constructed through the use of history and culture as 'Identity Tourism', which, according to her, becomes a medium to advance nationalism and national identity by exposing visitors to a national story by focusing on history and cultural distinctiveness. However, labelling any tourism attractions as such can be a troublesome issue, as there can be multiple discourses running through any touristic site or heritage attraction. Furthermore, touristic viewpoints do not remain constant but the 'gaze in any historical period is constructed in relationship to its opposite, to non-tourist forms of social experience and consciousness' (Urry, 2002: 1). This brings to light the fact that the reading of any attraction must be done within the socio-political context of the period studied.

One important aspect of social science from the perspective of research is that 'social context is crucial for the understanding of the social world and events and behaviours can have different meanings in different culture or historical eras' (Neuman, 2003: 146). Importantly, in terms of the nationalism debate, this is one of the highly charged contexts in Scotland, because: (i) it has recently achieved a long-time demand for a devolved parliament, and (ii) the Nationalists, whose ultimate aim is to gain full independence for Scotland, are in power. Amidst such a backdrop, it is imperative to see how tourism aids the 'national' sense by narrating the story of Scottish nationhood, not necessarily through political institutions or public policy but through various images and representations that tourists interact with while touring Scotland. I must mention that my emphasis in this book is not on nationalism in terms of a political unit, but as a cultural means through which people make sense of a nation. Thus, the nationalism I refer to in this book is a medium to express its distinctive national character – an idea that is strongly tied with Scotland.

Scotland and Nationalism

'Scottish nationalism is a phenomenon' (Hanham, 1968: 571) that has both a strong cultural component and a political realm that has started to express itself forcefully in recent years. Nationalism in Scotland can be examined at two levels: as a long-term phenomenon in Scottish life in which culture plays a crucial part, and in terms of the development of a nationalist movement and of the Nationalists' ideas and policy. I will now examine both of them in the following paragraphs. I must clarify here that it is not a remit of this book to see the political dimension of Scottish nationalism, but this dimension so often intersects with cultural aspects that it would be helpful to have a brief look at it.

Scottish nationalism from a cultural perspective

My argument rests on the important premise that assertion of Scottish distinctiveness – expressed through cultural authenticity and identity – is a form of nationalism. Nationalism for this purpose is understood as *'an ideological movement for attaining and maintaining autonomy, unity and identity on behalf of a population deemed by some of its members to constitute an actual or potential nation'* (Smith, 1991: 73, italics in original). I must consolidate this premise by offering further explanation. This is because nationalism defined as a striving towards unity and authenticity is contrary to the popular perception of nationalism that is understood as the political aspiration of a sovereign state: it is commonly deduced from the theories of nationalism that every nation must have its own state and for this reason nationalism is often seen as a political force. For sociologist Max Weber (1948), 'a nation is a community of sentiment which would adequately manifest itself in a state of its own; hence, a nation is a community which normally tends to produce a state of its own' (cited in Smith, 2008: 26).

However, there are a couple of problems with this approach. First, a strong political manifestation of Scottish nationalism is a relatively recent phenomenon. If we confine ourselves to the idea that nationalism is only a political force, that means we are implying that there was no nationalism in Scotland until the political manifestation of Scottish nationalism came to prominence; which, according to some scholars, happened after the war years, when southern (i.e. English) control or prospects of Empire faltered (Harvie, 1998). Second, linking demand for statehood with nationalism would be a very exclusionary concept in the Scottish case, as it would fail to acknowledge the vibrant nationalist movement that has always existed throughout Scottish history. It would be more appropriate to argue that the nationalist movement in Scotland has happened not necessarily as a resistance against the state of the Union but more as a claim to its cultural distinctiveness. This would also help us to understand Scottish nationalism more clearly as very often nationalism in Scotland transcends political aspirations alone. Nationalism in Scotland can be better comprehended if it is treated more as an assertion of a sense of Scottishness, its identity and authenticity. Accepting Scottish nationalism this way addresses two of its important features: (i) the centrality of culture in the theory of nationalism; (ii) that Scottish nationhood is much older than political nationalism, which has mobilised its cultural potency.

Culture has always assumed a strong place in the idea of nationalism. The conventional idea of nationalism is indeed the expression of fundamental, preordained cultural and social differences.

> We are led to imagine each group developing its cultural and social form in relative isolation, mainly in response to local ecologic factors, through a history of adaptation by invention and selective borrowing. This

> history has produced a world of separate peoples, each with their culture and each organised in a society which can legitimately be isolated for description as an island to itself. (Barth, 1981: 11, cited in McCrone, 2001: 50)

Though studying nationalism from different ideological backgrounds, scholars agree on one point, that culture provides the basic ingredient of nationalism. Gellner (1999) lays emphasis on cultural homogeneity in explaining nationalism. He argues that nationalism uses the pre-existing, historically inherited proliferation of cultures or cultural wealth, though it uses them selectively, and it most often transforms them radically. His idea is close to the one put forth by the influential theorist Anderson (1991), for whom nation is conceived as a deep horizontal relationship. According to Anderson, assertion of a common sense of identity is important in this imaging, to which museums, sacred sites and monuments were a medium to create an image of and spread the sense of community. But apart from national heritage, national movements could mobilise certain variants of feelings of collective belonging (Hobsbawm, 1999). Hobsbawm assigns this bond that could be language, religion, ethnicity and 'historical nation' as 'proto-national'.

Scotland has received considerable attention from the scholars of nationalism, all of whom place Scottish culture at the helm of nationalist ideology. What we can contend from this is that if the cultural sense makes the key component of Scottish nationalism, the mobilisation of cultural markers is essentially a form of nationalism. This argument may be at odds with some earlier researchers who have made different observations on the linkage between Scottish culture and Scottish nationalism; for example, David McCrone (1992: 174) takes the view that, 'unlike many forms of nationalism, the cultural content of the Scottish variety is relatively weak'. What he says about the Scottish nationalist movement is that the expression of political difference – a nationalism, if you want – has developed without the encumbrance of heavy cultural baggage. This does not necessarily mean that 'people of Scotland have forged an imagined community that eschews a cultural dimension' (Haesly, 2005: 254). Haesly (2005) has illustrated that culture is important to all types of Scottish identity. He argues that Scots may have different ideas about what constitutes Scottish culture, which is imaged heterogeneously by Scottish people in different regions; but 'these diverse Scottish individuals feel strongly enough about Scottish culture to include it as an important component of their national identity' (Haesly, 2005: 254).

Bechhofer and McCrone (2009) believe that being Scottish is not political or religious but more a cultural sense. That is why, according to them,

Scotland possesses and mobilises shared identity markers or a set of cultural symbols to assert the recognition and appreciation of Scotland's culture, its heritage, landscape and languages. Nairn (1981), for whom nationalism is a political force, sees it as a complex of events, feelings and ideas and a modern developmental phenomenon quite distinct from straightforward national and cultural differences. But he believes culture has played a major role in reinvigorating a sense of Scottish nationhood – which was one of the factors of political mobilisation that enabled the Scottish Nationalists to forge ahead in recent years.

From a slightly different perspective, Cohen (1996) assigns the primacy of Scottish selfhood and self-identity as 'personal nationalism'. That is, one can see the nation by looking at oneself. By looking at oneself, or one's experience, one's reading of history, perception of the landscape, reading of literature and music one can see the nation. It is on sharing personal experiences that sentiment and attachment to the nation are predicated. Thus, self-identity takes a very important role in the construction of nationalism. If Scottish nationalism gathered strength even during the virtues of the Union, according to Cohen (1996: 803), it is because Scottish nationalism 'appeared more as a lament for continuing denial of the integrity and authenticity of Scottish nationhood'.

The cultural sense of Scotland is older than the political manifestation seen in recent years. Scholars have argued that the occurrences of a sense of nationalism go further back, to the medieval period (Hasting, 1997). The historian Ferguson (1998) has shown that the origin of the Scottish nation can be traced back to the period after the fall of Roman Empire. For him, Scottish identity has been shaped by a complex amalgam of facts, myth and fanciful fable throughout history. According to Ferguson, Scottish national identity became more apparent during the long struggle for independence from 1286–1328, which heightened the perception of Scottish national identity. Amongst many other sources of identity, the distinctiveness of the Scottish royal line was used to counter English claims, and more emphasis was put by the Scots on their ancient lineage and the free monarchy that their ancestors had created. The Declaration of Arbroath is a strong testimony that asserted the existence of Scottish nationhood long before modern nations were believed to have been formed. The declaration condemned Edward I for his 'treacherous attack on the liberty of the Scots' and hailed Robert the Bruce, who rose to the defence of his country and struggled long and valiantly to restore the independence of Scotland. The declaration pronounced Robert the Bruce as its king by rightful succession and the 'consent of everyone of us'. The popular consent in the declaration testifies to the mark of the collective sense of that period.

The existence of Scottish nationhood and identity is also demonstrated by the presence of 'holy trinity' institutions at the time of the Union in 1707 (Davidson, 2000). The presence of the institutions of the Kirk, the education system and the law, all of which survived the Union, confirms that sense of Scottish national identity was strongly present during that time. The retention of these institutions would not have been possible had there been no sense of nationalism. Even after entering into the Union, Scotland's distinctiveness always remained separate and detached from English identity. Webster (1997) examines Scottish identity and argues that it is driven by its opposition to England. He argues that the making of Scottish national identity was largely the product of the medieval period that established its roots. According to Webster, this identity expressed itself in hostility to England. In his view, the identity of the Scottish nation came from a sense that Scotland is a country that came together in the Middle Ages and established itself in a long struggle against the threats of absorption by its more powerful and wealthy southern neighbour.

Scottish distinctiveness remained a vibrant form of nationalism in post-Union Scotland, now referred to as 'Unionist nationalism'. The strong sense of Scottish identity was very important in helping to keep Scottish nationhood alive despite its being part of the Union. It is a debatable issue whether Unionist nationalism was an assertion of Scottish distinctive culture and identity: it was an appreciation of the Union, but it also appreciated Scottish heritage (Mitchell, 1998). The historian Graeme Morton (1999) argues that a powerful sense of Scottishness was there during Victorian Scotland, despite the lack of political nationalism. The Unionist nationalists avidly took their position in defending Scottish identity on some occasions. For example, Sir Walter Scott in the 1820s, objecting to London's plan to abolish distinctive Scottish banknotes, believed that it was invoking the loss of national identity. He wrote, 'I think I see my native country of Scotland, if it is yet to be called by a title so discriminative, falling so far as its national, or rather, perhaps, I ought to say provincial, interests are concerned, daily more into more absolute contempt' (cited in McCrone, 2001: 44). Another example is his role in carefully choreographing the visit of King George IV to showcase Scottish distinctiveness and nationhood. Zuelow (2006) argues that the visit was used by Scott as a 'cultural translator', that is, through 'tartan' he translated his nationalist intent into a language that could be easily comprehended by all.

McCrone (2002) notes that Unionist nationalism became a driving force for the erection of the monuments to many of the Scottish nationalist icons. According to him, history was mobilised for political purposes while doing so, because the erection of most of the monuments marked their contribution to English heritage rather than that of Scotland. For example, the Walter Scott monument, the erection of which began in 1833, stressed Scott's contribution to English heritage. Those who raised funds for the erection of monuments to the two prime Scottish patriots – William Wallace and Robert the Bruce – did so by stressing the Union (McCrone, 2002). However, these monuments did not speak the language of the Union alone. Even the people who took the initiative did not always denigrate Scottish heritage. The Earl of Elgin, who took the chair at the inauguration of the 1856 movement to build the Wallace monument, said:

> if the Scottish people have been able to form an intimate union and association with a people more wealthy and more numerous than themselves, without sacrificing one jot of their neutral independence and liberty – these great results are due to the glorious struggle which was commenced on the plain of Stirling and consummated on that of Bannockburn... (Morton, 1993: 215)

The above expression of the Earl of Elgin shows that a sense of Scottish identity was deeply present even if it formed part of an appreciation of the Union. It suggests that Unionist nationalism did not mean dissipating Scottish nationhood with the Union. But it was a way of exemplifying Smith's (1991) idea of nationalism as an ideological movement for attaining and maintaining *autonomy*, *unity* and *identity* (emphasis in original).

Scottish nationalism as a 'nationalist' movement

Scotland is a nation that does not have a fully independent state. It has a vibrant independence movement that plays a major role in Scottish politics. This movement bears an intense significance for the Labour Party because the majority of Labour seats in the Westminster Parliament come from Scotland. In the Scottish Parliament, the Labour Party and the Scottish National Party (SNP) are major political contenders and the party politics of Scottish independence is mainly fought between them. The SNP is committed to full constitutional independence within the European Union. In this respect the SNP is different from other regionalist and nationalist parties, for example in Wales and Catalonia, which are committed to greater autonomy some way short of full independence (McCrone & Paterson, 2002). The devolution of the Scottish Parliament has remained an important element in Scotland since the 1960s. The Scottish Parliament was established in 1997, but nationalism still assumes greater significance in Scotland as the larger Nationalist goal to secure total independence still remains unfulfilled.

The Scottish independence movement has received unprecedented attention in post-devolution Scotland and the Nationalists have outperformed other parties in the consecutive two elections to the Scottish Parliament, in 2007 and, more robustly, in 2011.

The recent resurgence of nationalist politics in Scotland is the result of years of struggle. The origin of the strong 'national' feeling in Scotland could be said to date back to the 13th century after the death of Alexander III in 1286. His death did not bequeath direct royal rule, leading to a premature end to peace and stability in Scotland. What ushered in after that was a long period of conflict and strife with England. Pryde (1935: 264) writes, 'The bitter, prolonged and often sordid struggle evoked a grim determination to assert and maintain the national identity and inevitably imparted to it a definite colour of Anglophobia.' The resistance by Scottish heroes Robert the Bruce and William Wallace in defending Scotland from English occupation is recorded elsewhere (for Wallace see Cowan, 2007; for Bruce see Barrow, 1988). The apex of this struggle came in the form of the Declaration of Arbroath, which Cowan (2003) argues was the first national or governmental articulation in all of Europe and which strengthened the foundation of Scottish nationhood. So strong was the resistance against England that the declaration laid robust constraints on the king's power:

> Yet if he [the king] should give up what he has begun, seeking to make us or our kingdom subject to the king of England or the English, we would strive at once to drive him out as our enemy and a subverter of his own right and ours, and we would make some other man who was able to defend us our king. (Cowan, 2003: 146)

But in 1603, there was a Union of Crowns between the Kingdom of Scotland and England when the king of Scotland, James VI, succeeded to the throne of England on the death of Queen Elizabeth, as James I of England. A century later, in 1707, the Union of the Parliaments was signed, which created a legal entity of Great Britain. Despite formal incorporation into the Union, Scotland always possessed all the characteristics of a distinct nation, as the treaty gave certain guarantees to some of the Scottish institutions. The Scots retained their own church, and their own education and legal systems. Besides, they also have their own 'banking systems, their own system of central and local government, their own way of speaking English, and even their own Scottish Trades Union Congress' (Hanham, 1968: 571).

Scholars take the view that the years from the Union to the 20th century constituted a period of unparalleled prosperity for Scotland (Begg & Stewart, 1971). This relied on the success of coal, iron and steel, and shipbuilding as the basis of a booming Scottish economy. This period can be characterised by confidence in Scotland's contribution to the imperial partnership that was portrayed as a dynamic combination of Scottish and English prowess (Finlay, 1998). According to Finlay, the Scots provided the Union with some of its best soldiers, missionaries, explorers, scientists, engineers, businessmen, prime ministers and administrators. The period also marks the Scottish contribution to arts and literature that helped develop Scottish cultural identity, with authors such as Adam Smith, Sir Walter Scott and Robert Burns being accorded a place in the first rank of European writers (Begg & Stewart, 1971). Apart from the Jacobite rebellions of 1715 and 1745, strong dissent from the unionist consensus during that time was occasional and scattered.

Some scholars are of the opinion that modern Scottish nationalism has its roots in the 1850s and 1860s, when 'Scots were going through one of their periodic fits of vexation with the English' (Hanham, 1968: 572). According to Hanham, this was fostered by literary men whose main concern was to keep alive enthusiasm for the symbols of national culture – the exploits of Wallace and Bruce, the use of the Scottish flag and the Scottish coat of arms, the Scottish government offices and cultural institutions in Edinburgh. The main achievement of this movement was the erection of the towering Wallace monument at Abbey Craig near Stirling in the 1860s as a permanent reminder of the Scottish war of independence against English imperialism.

The Scottish political revival began in the 1880s when Gladstone's Midlothian campaigns in 1879 and 1880 for the first time since the Union made Scotland the focus of English party politics. According to Hanham (1968), Gladstone conceded the need for special attention to Scottish problems, and Scots began to assume that a future Liberal government would concede to them what Scotland had lacked since 1746: a Scottish Minister in cabinet with a Scottish Office to back up his endeavours. The Scottish Office came into being in 1885. Soon afterwards, Gladstone's adoption of home rule for Ireland gave a new impetus to nationalist sentiment and many Liberals began to champion a further measure of Scottish devolution. 'What they now wanted was the creation of a Scottish parliament of some sort and of a separate Scottish administration in Edinburgh to deal with exclusively Scottish affairs' (Hanham, 1968: 574).

By the turn of the 20th century, Scottish economic prosperity was waning and many radical supporters of the Liberal Party found themselves more in sympathy with the new Labour Party than with the Liberal and coalition governments in power at Westminster. The drift to Labour was made easier because the Labour Party in Scotland was at this time much more strongly nationalist than the Liberal Party had been. According to Hanham, since many of the Labour leaders had Irish nationalist connections which encouraged them to advocate a wide measure of home rule for Scotland and Ireland, the Labour Party appeared to promise many radicals what they wanted: this mix produced a new militant Scottish nationalism (1968: 575).

However, the nationalist fervour in the Labour Party of that time was secondary to its social welfare objectives. In the 20th century, the Union was sustained by empire and by welfare (Gamble, 2006). According to Gamble, the weakening of empire from the 1960s onward and of welfare from the 1970s onward was very disorienting for the British polity and its major parties. The overwhelming social and economic problems associated with the depression of the 1930s caused a steady decline in the appeal of Labour's nationalism. This paved the way for the creation of a united nationalist party. In 1928 a number of left-wing nationalist groups joined some students of the University of Glasgow to form the National Party of Scotland that in 1934 merged with the right-wing Scottish Party and was renamed the Scottish National Party (Hanham, 1968: 577). The new party aimed for total separation from the Union. The goal of the nationalists took a back seat because of the war years and also because between 1916 and 1945 neither the Liberal nor the Labour Party had a majority in the House of Commons, and the SNP was still in its infancy. Additionally, the rise of Labour following the introduction of universal suffrage in 1928 made the choice between capitalism and socialism the fundamental question of domestic politics for the next 60 years; other issues, including devolution and the constitution, received negligible attention (Gamble, 2006) – limited to a few efforts, such as the establishment of the Scottish Tourist Board in 1946.

Devolution and territorial politics became major issues in British domestic politics in the 1960s. This devolution debate took place in a very different context from the earlier devolution debate before 1914. The earlier Scottish Home Rule movement argued for the liberation of Scottish letters, arts and education from traditional subjection to English control and that a new Scottish culture be recreated by means of a revaluation, historical and critical, of the heritage of the past. It believed that, 'only by recapturing its nationhood in the fullest sense could Scotland make itself worthy and fit to receive the benefits of self-government' (Pryde, 1935: 278). But devolution in the 1960s was discussed in the context of Britain's likely membership of the European Community, and the numerous models of federal and devolved regional development elsewhere in Europe took on a new relevance, especially given the possibility that Europe itself might develop as a federal union (Gamble, 2006).

The SNP made significant policy changes after the war years, of which the most remarkable was the omission of a section on Scottish culture and more emphasis on the economy. This was an important policy departure because poets and writers had always prided themselves on being the backbone of the nationalist movement. The SNP's argument was that Scotland's consistently low rate of growth, relatively high unemployment, and high level of net emigration was the result of mismanagement by a predominantly English parliament (Begg & Stewart, 1971). The economic case for Scottish independence was not new, Pryde, in his paper as far back as 1935, notes that the nationalists believed that 'Scotland's salvation can be secured only by a national parliament that was in close touch with the country's economic needs and aptitudes, and in full control of its industrial life' (Pryde, 1935: 273). The discovery of North Sea oil in the 1970s gave an added impetus to the SNP's agenda. North Sea oil was crucial because it helped them challenge the idea that the country could not have independence without economic loss. Leaflets proclaiming, 'your choice – Poor British or Rich Scots' and the 1973 campaign 'It's Scotland's Oil' helped the SNP launch their case for economic independence (Lee, 1976). The breakdown of traditional 'cultural' party lines was also believed to have provided the Nationalists with an opportunity to replace class identity with national identity. Brand *et al.* (1994) believe that this is why national identity has gradually become an important force in Scottish politics, replacing traditional class divisions.

The industrial and political turmoil of the early 1970s meant that there was no immediate progress on plans for devolution, which had to wait for the Labour government that held office between 1974 and 1979. The Labour government was pressed by a growing nationalist threat in Scotland and Wales, the two areas that were key to Labour's prospects of winning an overall parliamentary majority in Westminster. Despite growing opposition within parties, the bill to hold referenda on the proposed new assembly was eventually passed, but the government's loss of an overall majority in parliament meant that the rebels in its ranks were able to amend the legislation (Gamble, 2006). The amendment crucially inserted a clause that made the result of the referendum valid only if 40% of the electorate voted for it. In Scotland the majority of those voting did vote 'Yes', but the number failed to cross the threshold.

The most potent catalyst to devolution came from the conservative government of Margaret Thatcher. The government relentlessly centralised power and drove through policies in regions, such as Scotland, that had not voted for them. Some scholars take the view that the reputation of the Thatcher government is a myth rather than reality, and have argued that Scotland and Wales were protected from the full force of the Thatcherite policies that were applied in England (Mitchell, 2003). For example, Stewart (2004) notes that for much of the 1980s the Scottish Secretary was George

Younger, who used his office to gain concessions and subsidies for Scotland in time-honoured fashion. There remained overall dissatisfaction over the Conservative government policies and a broad-based movement in civil society emerged to press for the restoration of the Scottish Parliament and the return of self-government. After 18 years of conservative rule, the Labour Party won the 1997 general election and agreed to the proposals for a Scottish Parliament.

There are various viewpoints as to why Labour in Scotland turned towards nationalism and agreed to a Scottish Parliament. Geekie and Levy (1989) assign two reasons. First, there is the office-seeking model, in which preclusion from power at Westminster generates the search for alternatives. In the case of Scottish Labour MPs, aspirant MPs and other career politicians, these opportunities were afforded by an elected assembly. Second, there is an ideology model, in which demands were fuelled by the legacy of the 'great devolution debate' of the 1970s and the general intellectual and organisational failure of the Labour Party to construct a serious alternative to 'Thatcherism'. However, there are other alternative explanations provided. For example, Hechter proposes an 'internal colonialism' model, which argues that nationalism in the Celtic fringes has traditionally been expressed via a disproportionate anti-Conservative vote (Hechter, 1975).

After the election of the Labour government in Westminster, a referendum was held in September 1997 in which 74.3% of those who voted approved the devolution plan. The Westminster Parliament subsequently approved the Scotland Act 1998 which created an elected Scottish Parliament with control over most domestic policies. The Act sets out its powers as a devolved legislature. It defines the legislative competence of the parliament – the areas in which it can make laws – by explicitly specifying powers that are reserved to the Westminster Parliament of the United Kingdom. Importantly, all matters that are not explicitly reserved are automatically the responsibility of the Scottish Parliament. The Westminster Parliament reserves the right to amend the terms of reference of the Scottish Parliament, and can extend or reduce the areas in which it can make laws. Westminster also retains the power to abolish the Scottish Parliament and the Welsh Assembly by a simple majority vote in both houses, but since both were sanctioned by referenda, Gamble (2006) takes the view that it would be politically difficult to abolish them without the sanction of a further vote by the people.

The development of Scottish devolution shows that there are three distinctive features of the Scottish movement: (i) it is a peaceful movement and has followed a constitutional path; (ii) it is pro-Europe and (iii) it is grounded in economic terms. The late Neil MacCormick, who was the vice-president of the SNP, an SNP Member of the European Parliament, and was for many years involved in SNP constitutional policy-making, noted that a rigorous constitutionalism has always characterised the SNP's approach to its central policy objective of re-establishing Scotland as an independent state (MacCormick, 2000). He argued that the Union, which was constitutionally achieved in 1707, is one that can equally constitutionally be dissolved by appropriate measures, should the political will to do so be exercised. Scottish nationalism as it is now is closely pro-Europe (Pittock, 2008). The SNP officially adopted the 'independence in Europe' slogan in 1988. It clarified,

> Independence in Europe means accepting the role and responsibilities of a member state of the European Union who have pooled certain of their sovereign rights for common advantage. Sharing sovereignty in Europe in this way enhances Scotland's sovereignty because it increases our influence. (*The Morning Star*, 2007)

Ichijo (2004) argues that the pro-Europe stance of the SNP is a way to express Scottish uniqueness and this is where Scotland differs from England, which is not a keen supporter of the European Union.

The SNP's line of argument for independence is based on economic terms: that Scotland can be better off with economic independence. However, this basis for independence was severely shattered in 2008 as The Royal Bank of Scotland and HBOS, the twin pillars of Scotland's economy, were largely taken over by the Westminster government, questioning the very basis of the SNP's argument for independence. Rayner and Kirkup (2008) write, 'without financial independence, Scotland could not have political separation from the rest of the United Kingdom, and the question of whether Scotland could ever stand on its own two feet has been brought into sharp focus'. Despite Scotland's economic vulnerability as shown during the banking crisis, the SNP managed to achieve electoral success in 2011. This sheds light on the complex nature of the interaction between national identity and political attitude in Scotland. Support for independence and support for the SNP do not necessarily mean the same thing, as Bond and Rosie (2002: 43) have noted, 'a large minority of SNP supporters do *not* support independence' (emphasis in original).

The nationalism movement in Scotland has not subsided but has been elevated to a new level after the devolution of power, giving a strong boost to the Nationalists. The previously adjourned parliament resumed session in 1999 for the first time since 1707 after the election selected Labour as the largest party. The Labour Party and the Liberal Democrats formed a government – also called the Scottish Executive. The 2003 election to the second

Scottish Parliament brought no change in terms of control of the Scottish Executive. However, the third election in 2007 raised the SNP to the single largest party and brought them to power with support from the Green Party on certain issues. The fourth general election of the Scottish Parliament in 2011 has been the most notable one. The SNP now has an overall majority of 69 out of 129 seats and around 45% of all votes cast – enough to hold a referendum on independence from the United Kingdom. What is noteworthy is that the election delivered the first majority government since the opening of the parliament. This is remarkable because Scotland uses the mixed member proportional representation system to elect members of the Scottish Parliament (MSPs) that was originally planned to prevent single-party governments, mainly the Nationalists. Such was the scale of their gains in the election that, of the 73 constituencies in Scotland, only 20 are now represented by MSPs of other political parties. After assuming office as the first minister, the leader of the SNP, Alex Salmond, took no time to make clear his intention to hold an independence referendum in the year 2014.

In terms of tourism, MacLellan (2010) has pointed out that devolution has brought about some changes in the institutional structure of tourism in Scotland. He notes that tourism has come under scrutiny by successive ministers and administrations and there has been some policy intervention. These can be found in the various documents of the Scottish government – *Tourism Framework For Action 2000* followed by *Tourism Framework for Action 2002–2005* and then *Scottish Tourism: The Next Decade – A Tourism Framework For Change* (Scottish Executive, 2006). The establishment of the parliament has provided a platform for debate and allowed opposition parties to put forward views on tourism that range from moderate calls to streamline structures, to gaining independence from the British Tourism Authority by forming Area Tourism Boards (ATBs) direct from the Scottish Tourist Board (STB), to more radical changes such as having a separate Minister for Tourism and taking powers from the STB and passing them to the Scottish Enterprise Network (Kerr & Wood, 1999, cited in MacLellan, 2010).

Most notably, the STB received close attention in the post-devolution period. After a series of studies and consultations (see Lennon & Hay, 2003; Hay, 2007) the overall structure of the STB and ATBs has been overhauled and all ATBs merged into one organisation. In 2001 the STB became VisitScotland and in 2005 it became a single, countrywide comprehensive organisation managing all 120 Tourism Information Centres in Scotland, with 14 regional offices and its own offices in London, Edinburgh and Inverness (MacLellan, 2010). In 2005, the Scottish Executive published another document concerning Scottish Tourism – *Scottish Tourism: The Next Decade – A Tourism Framework for Change* (Scottish Executive, 2006) – that envisages growing tourism revenue by 50% in the 10 years to 2015. It places important emphasis on the need for business to take the lead for product development and innovation, on sustainable development, and for integrated marketing. The first Nationalist government identified tourism as one of the six main priority industries as key growth sectors. Significantly, it also went ahead with the tourism mega-event 'Year of Homecoming' throughout 2009, announced by its Labour government predecessor, which MacLellan (2010) notes, had a number of minor and innocuous initiatives for the nationalistic promotion of Scotland. Scottish devolution, as discussed above, is the background against which this book must be read and analysed, but the object of my inquiry is images, icons and objects that bestow tourists with the cultural impression of the Scottish nation.

I must also clarify here that despite my assertion that a sense of cultural distinctiveness or identity is a form of nationalism, my contention is not of cultural nationalism as such. The primary aim of cultural nationalists is to revive what they regard as a distinctive and primordial collective personality which has a name, unique origin, history, culture, homeland and social and political practices (Hutchison, 1999). We will see in this book that some of the actors in tourism do see Scottish heritage and icons in a similar way to the above. But I acknowledge Hutchinson (1999), who believes that Scottish nationalism is a nationalistic reaction that follows from a particular perception of the denigration of a culture by a powerful neighbour or 'the other'. I differ from the view that cultural nationalism as a movement is distinct from that of political nationalism. I agree with Hutchinson that nationalism is a political movement and that it clearly has a cultural dimension which may help achieve the broader political goals. The cultural dimension of nationalism has great importance in Scotland, because in the contemporary milieu, as McCrone *et al.* (1995: 182) point out, it is becoming more 'difficult to separate cultural and political realms in modern Scotland'. They argue that the use of heritage is increasingly becoming political because respondents increasingly associate it with a strong sense of lineage and inheritance. Heritage has the power to define who one is in a historical sense, which can be meaningful politically (McCrone *et al.*, 1995; Urry 2006). For instance, Edensor (1997a) has shown how the Bannockburn Heritage Centre evokes political significance.

However, this does not mean that heritage has to acquire a political worth to evoke nationalistic sentiment. As has been noted earlier, we should not see the Scottish sense of identity entirely grounded on political aspirations alone. Bechhofer and McCrone (2009) argue that Scottish nationalism is a statement of identity, the potency of which is separable from – and independent of – its more partisan political programme. In this context,

Nairn's (1997) view is clearer. He makes note of two strands of nationalism in Scotland, what he calls: uppercase nationalism and lowercase nationalism: the first representing the specific political demand for a nation-state, and the latter a more general identification with the Scottish people, compatible with a variety of political positions. He places both under the heading of nationalism. According to Nairn (1995), alongside partisan Scottish Nationalism, ('uppercase' nationalism), there is a very widespread 'lowercase' nationalism which crosses party lines; and this transcends the political division between nationalists and so-called unionists. Throughout this book the term 'nationalism' refers to the cultural dimension of nationalism, or lowercase nationalism, unless otherwise stated: the political importance of this, however, cannot be ruled out. In the next chapter we will look into the role of tourism in creating a distinctive identity of Scotland both as a nation and a destination.

3 Scottish Identity in Tourism

Introduction

Tourism has portrayed a distinctive image of Scotland, resting very much on its landscape, history and cultural heritage. This image has been reinforced for almost two centuries by a peculiar combination of geography, emigration, social stratification, romantic appeal and attachment in literature and art (Butler, 1998). Mountains, tartan and kilts, bagpipes, castles, Highland dancing, haggis, heather, golf, Balmoral Castle and lochs or lakes are the most prominent Scottish images. The combination of these images has conferred a distinctive tourism identity on Scotland. In this chapter I will show that tourism as a booster of these images has played an important part in the manifestation of Scottish identity, that touristic representation of Scotland is replenished with identifiers of Scotland. The production of Scotland through the framing of identity is important because identity assumes a very special significance in Scottish nationalism.

My argument here is not to question or acknowledge the appropriateness of representing Scotland through these identifiers, which can be a separate issue, but I recognise the centrality of identity in Scottish tourism. My contention is that Scottish tourism is largely an affirmation of Scottish identity which resonates positively with the Scottish sense of nationalism as noted in the earlier chapter. Identity is so strongly linked to Scottish tourism that it has formed powerful images to identify with Scotland, and tourism has developed and revolved around those areas and objects that are identifiers of Scotland. Many of these identifiers were always there and predate the arrival of tourism, but tourism largely exploited these identifiers to produce Scotland to the visitors. For instance, images of tartan and bagpipes are strong markers of Scottish identity and Scotland is now deeply epitomised by its landscapes and places, such as the Scottish Highlands and Edinburgh. This chapter intends to show the instrumental role of tourism in producing Scotland through narratives and icons that are referent of its identity, and assumes significance in the manifestation and dissemination of Scottish nationalism.

The production of identity through tourism is not new and has been well-recognised by scholars (Burns, 2004; Burns & Novelli, 2006). Tourism can play a very important role in the portrayal of a distinctive national image (D. Hall, 2002; Kotler & Gertner, 2002; Olins, 2002). Kotler and Gertner (2002) take the view that a country's image results from its geography, history, proclamations, art and music, famous citizens and other features. As tourism is a sphere where 'ideological framing of history, nature, and tradition' (MacCannell, 1992: 1) takes place in various forms, it has an influence in the construction and promotion of distinctive national identity. For instance, Hughes argues that tourism since its beginning has been framing a particular way of seeing Scotland (Hughes, 1992). Others have noted that the 'production' of Scotland by visitors, or seeing Scotland, has happened through various narratives and representations in tourism (see Durie, 2003; Gold & Gold, 1995; Grenier, 2005). Grenier (2005: 29) notes that 'the role of many travel accounts, diaries, letters, and sketches produced by visitors was not just to make Scotland known, but to interpret, to make sense of place'.

The ubiquity of tourism and with it the symbols and images of Scotland it portrays gives a distinctive sense of Scotland to visitors. The development of all of these symbols and images did not happen together but occurred at different historical periods and was the product of social construction (Gold & Gold, 1995; Hughes, 1992). The touristic production of the iconography of Scotland also created a way of viewing Scotland. For example, Hughes (1992) opines that the dominant perception of Scotland still retains the legacy of Victorian ways of seeing, though lately a different perspective has also become ascendant. Gold and Gold (1995: 11) argue that the iconography of tourism images has remained contextual because tourism promoters avail themselves of a vast range of symbols and ideas that they can recycle and transform when communicating with their potential audience. We will see later that the development of Scotland as a destination is a culmination of various narratives and attractions; it is spread across wider activities and a wider period, and these developments have shaped the distinctive sense of Scotland.

I will look into the trends in the nature of the development of Scottish tourism by dividing it into three evolutionary trends – though some of the developments happen at the same time and tend to overlap each other. The period from the 18th century to the early 19th century is taken as an initial phase when Scotland was visited by the first travellers. Their travel accounts introduced Scotland to the outer world and provided it with the image of a wild, untamed and fearsome country. The work of Sir Walter Scott and the subsequent period is taken as the second phase. It is in this period that Scotland witnessed the influx of mass tourism which resulted in the development of a varied product base in Scotland. This was the time when the country's image diversified and newer markers of Scotland were developed. Yet tourism largely revolved around the Scottish Highlands that reiterated Highland culture as the marker of Scottish identity. The period from the mid-20th century can be considered as a third phase, wherein tourism is more diversified and discrete and when disparate identities have become more prominent. Destinations are creating their own niche markets and promoting their own identities, arising out of a need for product differentiation and competition. However, what is also evident is that the touristic image of Scotland remains the same, based on the traditional image that puts Scottish nature and landscape at the centre to produce the imagery of Scotland.

Formation of Scotland's Identity

Travellers' accounts made the greatest contribution in the development of tourism in Scotland, as they played a very influential role in the way Scotland was 'viewed'; and the image of the country presented in them remained a guide for other visitors in subsequent years. Durie (2012: 11) writes that 'were it not for the journals and diaries specially kept by visitors during their travels, or as summer sections in yearly journals, or the letters sent home or to friends, we would know little indeed about tourism in premodern Scotland'. Many parts of the country until the start of 18th century largely remained relatively unknown to outsiders and there was very limited information about the Scottish Highlands. The travel accounts of those who visited Scotland during the early 18th century mostly speak of the country almost with 'horror, as a black howling wilderness, full of bogs and boulders, mostly treeless, and nearly unfit for human habitation' (Youngson, 1974: 13). The severity of travel features prominently in almost all accounts. Importantly, the image of the country presented by the visitors was mainly dominated by their impression of the Scottish Highlands. In order to comprehend the image of Scotland created or presented in the travel accounts of early travellers, I will look into the prominent and influential accounts of Pennant, Daniel Defoe, Samuel Johnson and James Boswell and Dorothy Wordsworth. The image of the country presented in these early travel accounts remained a guide for other visitors in subsequent years, giving Scotland an identity as a wild and sublime country.

The Jacobite rebellions of 1715 and 1719 created an initial interest in Scotland and were important in drawing visitors, mostly to the Highlands.

But 'Ossian' is considered one of the first examples of the phenomenon of tourists being enticed to Scotland. Places apparently mentioned by 'Ossian' and touched by the magic associated with his mystical vision of the Celtic past lured initial travellers. Macpherson's 'Ossian' poems, published in 1760, created an early inquisitiveness about Scotland. Leneman (1987), for example, claimed that the 'Ossian' poetry had a three-fold effect. First, it gave people a new way of looking at sublime, wild and desolate scenery. Second, it encouraged them to view landscape in association with Ossian, peopling the landscape with their imagination. Finally, it supplied a new way of seeing the Highlander. Gold and Gold (1995: 54) are of the opinion that Macpherson's writings played a part in the emerging sense not only of British identity, but of a growing sense of nationalism in Europe.

The early accounts were written mostly by either English travellers or for English readers, with the exception of Boswell. Later travellers followed the trend and presented Scotland to the outside world as a savage, dreadful country. The picture of Scotland presented in these accounts remained uniform, though the narration varied according to the writer's background, interests and purpose of travel. For example, the travel account of Defoe (1971), who travelled in the year 1729, is written from the English perspective. This is unsurprising given his background as an English spy. While presenting Scotland to an English audience he creates Scotland as the 'other', a distinctive entity from England. He writes,

> the first town we come to is perfectly Scots, as if you were 100 miles north of Edinburgh; nor is there the least appearance of anything English, either in customs, habits, usages of the people, or their way of living, eating, dress, or behaviour; or any more than if they had never heard of an English nation, was there an Englishman to be seen, or an English family to be found among them. (Defoe, 1971: 564)

This 'othering' of Scotland is visible throughout his account. He presents the Scottish Highlands as a 'frightful country', full of wilderness.

Defoe's underlying motive to stress and bolster the Union is visible in his conspicuous justification of the inevitability of the act of Union and its benefits:

> Scotland is now established in a lasting tranquillity, the wars between the nations are at an end, the washings and plunderings, the ravages and blood are all over; the lands in Scotland will now be improved, their estates double; the charges of defending her abroad and at her home lies upon England; the taxes are easy and ascertained, and the West-India

> trade abundantly pour in wealth upon her; and this all true; and, in the end, I am still of opinion Scotland will be gainer. (1971: 637)

He portrays Scots as less industrious than English people and tries to support the Union wherever possible. For him the benefits of commerce obtained by Scotland through the Union appear visible by opening the trading door to English colonies. His account is more a description of the state of trade and commerce and is less specific to the interest of travellers. He also mentions palaces, castles and forts throughout his tour and notices the richness of fine palaces compared to those of most princes in Europe or England, though the question might have been asked how these palaces could be so rich if Scotland were poor and the Scots indolent. His role as an English spy might have played a part in his narrative of Scotland.

Pennant travelled to various parts of Scotland in 1769. He was an English naturalist and gave the first account of the country that presented a grim image of Scotland as a wild untamed country inhabited by savage people, starting straight at the border. This is how he introduces his account of first entering the country:

> The entrance in Scotland has a very uncompromising look; for it wanted, for some miles, the cultivation of the parts more distant from England: but the borders were necessarily neglected; for, till the accession of James VI and even long after, the national enmity was kept up, and the borders of both countries discouraged from improvement, by the barbarous inroads of each nation. (Pennant, 1776: 30–31)

His views on its inhabitants were grim. He viewed them as a lazy, warrior class of people. According to him the Scottish people were:

> ... indolent to a high degree, unless roused to war, from experience, to lend any disinterested assistance to the distressed traveller, either in directing him on his way, or affording their aid in passing the dangerous torrents of the Highlands ... (Pennant, 1776: 127)

The most influential travel narrative is the separate accounts of the joint travels of Samuel Johnson and James Boswell (1984, Johnson's account originally published in 1775 and Boswell's in 1786). Johnson's account of the Western Isles tell us more about the people and society. It gives a traveller's account of the Scottish Highlands – until then considered 'terra incognita'. Johnson's journal was important in dispelling the hostile perception of the Highland people whilst acknowledging the wilderness of the area's landscape. Upon entering the Highlands they declare, 'we were now to bid farewell to the luxury of travelling, and to enter a country upon which perhaps no wheel has ever rolled' (1984: 52). Despite this natural wilderness, Johnson acknowledges the hospitable nature of its inhabitants. He remarks, 'Civility seems part of the national character of Highlanders. Every chieftain is a monarch, and politeness, the natural product of royal government, is diffused from the laird through the whole clan' (1984: 52). Yet he also tried to present savageness, if anything, as the product of their situation rather than character, '... for the manners of mountaineers are commonly savage, but are rather produced by their situation than derived from their ancestors' (1984: 63). His account was instrumental in presenting the Highlands as a safe and secure place for travelers: 'thirty years ago no herd had ever been conducted through the mountains, without paying tribute in the night, to some of the clans, but cattle are now driven, and passengers travel without danger, fear, or molestation' (1984: 64). In another instance he reiterates the state of safety achieved through the law that regulated traditional Highland society: '... there is now happily an end to all fear or hope from malice or from favour. The roads are secure in those places through which, forty years ago, no traveller could pass without a convoy' (1984: 100).

The travel accounts by Johnson and Boswell respectively tried to answer many questions on Highland culture and way of life. The accounts of their travels in 1769 tried to dispel the perception of the Highland people as savages and profoundly acknowledged the recent changes in Scotland's culture and society.

> There was perhaps never any change of national manners so quick, so great, and so general, as that which has operated in the Highlands, by the last conquest, and the subsequent laws. We came thither too late to see what we expected, a people of peculiar appearance, and a system of antiquated life. The clans retain little now of their original character, their ferocity of temper is softened, their military ardour is extinguished, their dignity of independence is depressed, their contempt of government subdued and their reverence of their chiefs abated. (1984: 73)

The above comment serves to create an inquisitiveness about the Scottish Highlands, a desire to visit them before it is too late. While acknowledging that they are losing their essence, they also acknowledge that much of the authentic Highlands has survived.

> The highland lords made treaties, and formed alliances, of which some traces may *still* be found, and some consequences *still* remain as lasting evidences of petty regality. (1984: 66, emphasis added)

The journals also tried to showcase the variety within Scotland, indicating that Scotland was not a homogeneous unit but a combination of diverse cultural and natural landscapes. They also show the intensity of difference within Scotland.

> To the southern inhabitants of Scotland, the state of the mountains and islands is equally unknown with that of Borneo or Sumatra. Of both they have only heard a little, and guess the rest. They are strangers to the language and the manners, to the advantages and wants of the people, those life they would model, and whose evils they would remedy. (1984: 96)

An important account of Scotland during that time comes from Dorothy Wordsworth, who toured Scotland in the year 1803. Wordsworth's account (1997, original publication 1894) was the first romantic narrative of Scotland. Romanticism was a movement that viewed emotion as an authentic source of aesthetic experience. It placed a new emphasis on emotions such as trepidation, horror, terror and awe. The emotions experienced in confronting the sublimity of untamed nature and its picturesque qualities were the new aesthetic categories. Wordsworth portrays Scotland as a country of nature that was untouched and full of wilderness, where houses and inns were notoriously lacking in comforts and amenities and cleanliness. As she puts it, '... many of the gentlemen's houses which we have passed in Scotland have an air of neglect and even of desolation' (Wordsworth, 1997: 44). Her account stresses Scotland's distinctiveness as a romantic country. She feels this distinctiveness as soon as she enters it, 'we now felt indeed we were in Scotland; there was a natural peculiarity in this place. In the scenes of the Nith it had not been the same as England, but yet not simple, naked Scotland' (1997: 48).

The appeal of Scotland as a romantic nation is ubiquitous in her account, which was in tune with the period that viewed Romanticism as a hallmark of enjoying nature. Scottish nature was a perfect place to visit, she says 'I must say, however, that we hardly ever saw a thoroughly pleasing place in Scotland, which had not something of wilderness in its aspects of one sort or other' (Wordsworth, 1997: 143).

It was a perfect place for an imaginative visitor to experience their pleasures. It also presented the people of Scotland in such a way that their underdevelopment and pastoral life were seen in a positive light by a romantic visitor. For example, she writes, 'there are so many inhabited solitudes, and the employments of the people are so immediately connected with the places where you find them, and their dresses so simple, so much alike, yet, from their being folding garments, admitting of an endless variety, and falling often so gracefully' (Wordsworth, 1997: 55).

Wordsworth describes Loch Lomond as an 'outlandish scene' (Wordsworth, 1997: 87). For her the region as a whole 'was a combination of natural wilderness, loveliness, beauty, and barrenness, or rather bareness, yet not comfortless or cold; but the whole was beautiful' (Wordsworth, 1997: 88). Her account also played a good part in dispelling some of the older curiosities about the inhabitants, '... we were not afraid of trusting ourselves to the hospitality of the Highlanders ...' (Wordsworth, 1997: 136).

All of these travel accounts portrayed the image of Scotland as a country of wilderness; of untamed and sublime nature; of a lack of amenities; with indolent yet hospitable and pleasing inhabitants. An observation can be made that most of these accounts were written by well-known literary figures who visited Scotland with a distinct purpose. A question arises: did that view belong to a specific kind of 'elite' visitor, or was it the same across the board? Durie (2012) brings us the stories of Scotland narrated by 'ordinary' travellers in their personal journals, diaries and letters in the 18th and 19th centuries and gives us a glimpse of the historical period and the changing nature of tourists' behaviour and its effect on the organisation of tourism. Durie (2012: 31) largely conforms to what has already been revealed about Scotland; that is, his collection also speaks of the country with horror, as a black howling wilderness, full of bogs and boulders, a dreadful desert, 'without tree, any mark of cultivation or face, human or beastly'.

The travel accounts also gave a comparison and distinction between Scotland and England and within Scotland between Highland and Lowland. They portrayed the Scottish Highlands as a country having distinctive cultures and societies of its own. The meticulous descriptions of some of the places helped create a curiosity about Scotland and at the same time helped forge a distinctive Scottish identity based on the image portrayed, creating Scotland as 'the other', worthy of touristic consumption. Most importantly, the identity of Scotland as a destination in the later periods rested on the image created during this period.

Period of Composite Identity

Tourism flourished henceforth and the nature of touristic consumption was instrumental in producing a distinctive sense of Scotland. The consumption of tourism was the result of the contributions of Sir Walter Scott and royalty, later commercially exploited by Thomas Cook. The combination of Celtic heroes, Highland scenery, chivalry, fine emotions and sensibility led to new ways of seeing and representing the Scottish landscape (Gold & Gold, 1995). Butler (1985) has presented a detailed account of how tourism evolved in the Scottish Highlands. According to him, the arrival of 'the romantic traveller' and 'the aristocratic sportsman', including the writings of Sir Walter Scott, drew unprecedented attention to the land, particularly the Highlands.

The contribution of Sir Walter Scott was immense in the development of modern tourism in Scotland, he created an immense touristic interest in the country. Paterson (1965: 147) writes, '... for thousands of people both during his lifetime and after his death, it was his [Scott's] writing which provided their introduction to the Scottish landscape. Whatever else may be disputed about Scott's career, virtual unanimity exists that he was the father of the Scottish tourist trade.' The great popularity of Scott's works, many of which romanticised the scenery and inhabitants of the Highlands, resulted in changing people's perceptions of the area. Murdoch (1852: 324) notes 'when Scott adopted the Highlands as the subject of romantic story and song... then began a new era of comfort in every spot which his magic touched'. Though Scott has been accused of romanticising the Scottish Highlands, his writing was not exclusively concerned with that area. He gave equal treatment to all regions, but the bulk of his descriptions were devoted to the Highlands. For instance, central Scotland, the south-west and the Border region were the settings of some of his later novels, but he rarely described them (Paterson, 1965). More than his writing, Scott's role during King George's 1822 visit to Edinburgh was greatly instrumental in recreating Highland identity. His attempt to 'restore Scottish pride and identity' made an important contribution to the creation of Scottish identity. He persuaded the king to appear dressed in tartan: to a certain class of people this was a visual representation of national unity cast in Highland clothing, an act that helped conflate the Scottish and Highland identity (Gold & Gold, 1995: 83). Gold and Gold (1995) believe that Scott's works made visitors feel that they needed to visit the Highlands to see the 'authentic' Scotland.

However there were other important artists and literary figures such as Turner, the noted English artist; William Scrape, a landed gentleman and amateur artist; the writings of Burns, Wordsworth, Dickens and Tennyson, who all visited various parts of the Highlands; their works, while small in importance compared to those of Scott, added further literary respectability to a visit to the area. The drastic improvement in steam engines helped the appeal created by these writers to materialise into travel by hugely improving the speed, comfort and safety of access to these areas, or at least parts of them (Thomas, 1965, cited in Butler, 1998).

Royalty also made a tremendous boost to tourism during the period (Durie, 2003). Queen Victoria and Prince Albert annually holidaying in the

Dee Valley helped to change the perception of Scotland and its tourism. Albert participated in stalking at Drummond and in Glen Tilt. '(B)y spending every autumn at Balmoral, the Queen and her husband probably did contribute to the general romantic enthusiasm of the Victorians for mountains and far places: and so in an oblique fashion, they may have increased still further the drift of the well-to-do southerners towards the Scottish moors' (Hart-Davis, 1978: 125). The purchase of Balmoral and the travels of the Queen around the Highlands and Islands gave social approval to the idea of a summer estate in the Highlands of Scotland, resulting in increased numbers of visitors from that date and the purchase of estates, a process which is still continuing to the present day and which shows no sign of declining.

In the same period Thomas Cook started to modernise tourism. By appreciating the importance of railway travel, he transformed the Highlands' image from wild and untamed to a more acceptable and welcoming place. He pointed out in answer to the question 'Is it safe and proper for ladies to join in Highland tours¿' that the majority of his patrons had in fact been ladies (Cook, 1861: 36). Cook continued to market Scotland on the basis of the appeal created by Sir Walter Scott, but soon broadened the geographical base of his tours to other areas as he saw their potential for attracting visitors (Cook, 1861). This helped '... fresh spatial patterns emerge and new destinations within Scotland developed' (Butler, 1998), in which the railways played a major part. The railway was important in opening up a picturesque and interesting portion of Scotland and in attracting many thousands of tourists annually to famous places and districts (Groome, 1894: Vol. IIh, 268).

The development of rail services had enabled efficient links to be made with existing steamer services, and helped some centres to grow markedly in importance with respect to tourism, mostly as transit or link destinations. This helped in developing individual destinations within the travel routes. According to Butler (1985), these included places like Inverness: with 'a large number of excellent Hotels ... [Inverness was] ... a centre for tourists and sportsmen' (Groome, 1894: Vol. IV, 281). Small burghs such as Fortrose (linked by railway in 1893), Cromarty and Rosemarkie began to develop tourist industries, capitalising on their dry climate and sandy beaches. To the west, Strathpeffer was further stimulated in 1911 by the opening of the Highland Railway's Hotel and the addition of a special summer 'Strathpeffer Express', which ran until 1915 (Valiance, 1972: 99). North of the Black Isle, other east coast settlements in Ross and Cromarty began to develop a tourist trade. By 1894 Tain had several hotels, and the extension of services eventually to Wick and Thurso allowed the Sutherland villages, such as Brora and Golspie, to exploit their coastal situation. These were the most significant developments. Butler (1998) writes that because of these developments Scotland became not one generalised destination, but a series of destinations, often clearly defined and aggressively targeted to specific markets.

If the growth of industry is any indication, sport became a considerable motivation for visitors. At the end of the 19th century there were approximately 170 inns and hotels in the Highlands and Islands (Butler, 1985). Their distribution reflected the orientation of the tourist industry in 1894 towards sporting activities, and the few tourist centres which existed at that time. The development of fishing, shooting and golf facilities is evidence of this. The reputation of the Highlands and Islands for fishing was as high, or higher. Catches of fish were often spectacular: at Kildonan, 'three men in five days killed with the fly, 600 trout, weighing over 400 lbs' (Groome, 1894: Vol. IV, 361).

For Hart-Davis (1978), the period from 1880–1910 was the heyday of Highland stalking, caused in part by an increasing demand for sport, and partly by a decline in mutton and wool prices, allowing more land to come under deer rather than sheep. Stalking was an almost exclusively upper-class sport (Hart-Davis, 1978: 163). Severe opposition to attempts to open up the countryside to the public at large, such as the unsuccessful Access to the Mountains Bill in 1885, was quickly voiced. O'Dell and Walton (1962: 333) record 1912 as the year in which deer forest acreage reached its maximum of 3,858,000 acres, with 203 forests in existence (Butler, 1985).

Also in the mid-19th century, a new system of water treatment, or hydropathy, arrived and quickly became fashionable in Britain. It took strong root in Scotland because its locations provided an ideal environment for relaxing and revitalising (Durie *et al.*, 2006). These hydros were spread across Scotland. In the Scottish Borders there were three (Moffat, Peebles and Melrose); on the west coast another three (Kyles of Bute, Shandon and Seamill); in the central belt and Perthshire four (Dunblane, Callander, Crieff and Pitlochry); and in the north-east at Forres and Deeside. According to Durie, the appeal of the curative regime, which involved baths, showers and massage, was enhanced in the Scottish hydros by a firm emphasis on temperance, diet, fresh air and exercise.

The rateable or assessed value of the shooting and fishing was considerable also, and played an important role in the economy of the Highland counties. The preservation of the Highland landscape as deer forest matched the image of the Highlands in the minds of both the romantic traveller and the mass tourist, and indeed the 20th-century tourist. Tourist guides published in the late 19th century refer to fishing opportunities, if less so to deer stalking possibilities (Ward & Lock, 1880). Young's *Angler's and Sketcher's Guide to Sutherland* (1881: 108) notes that one shooting lodge in Lochinver was converted to a hotel offering shooting and fishing for 60 tourists. Young's guide is interesting as it is one of the earliest references to golf links, now a major attraction for many visitors to Scotland.

Fishing and shooting, particularly the latter, were very much the privilege of the few. The amount of money required to partake in activities was beyond the reach of the vast majority of the population. The relatively high cost of travel, and the time involved, the generally expensive nature of most of the accommodation, and, at least until the early 20th century, the absence of holidays with pay, meant that for the most part the Highlands and Islands remained the holiday area of a fortunate elite and were not subjected to the pressures of large numbers of visitors.

In the Scottish Lowlands the growth and development of Abbotsford was remarkable in the 19th century. Though Abbotsford had become a favourite port of call for many visitors during Sir Walter Scott's lifetime, after his death in 1832 it speedily became a literary and historical shrine, drawing a large number of visitors to see the house, inspect Scott's study and library, and examine the antiquarian relics and treasures that Scott had collected (Durie, 1992). The growth of Abbotsford helped tourism around the Borders region, involving Melrose and Dryburgh Abbeys, Ettrick and Yarrow. There was also an increased visitor trend to the Burns Monument in Alloway near Ayr. Most of the visitors to Ayr were from Scotland, whereas in Abbotsford almost 35–40% of the visitors were from outside Scotland (Durie, 1992).

The development of tourism was instrumental in creating a sense of Scotland. The nature and place of destinations, attractions and activities produced Scotland for the travellers. The development of tourism in the later periods influenced and established these images as distinctive of Scotland. Two key points must be noticed here in terms of identity reinforcement: (i) diversification of tourism – both in terms of product base and visitor profile; and (ii) the establishment of the Highlands image as typical of Scotland. The diversification of tourism meant Scotland witnessed increasing participation and its tourism product base started to change. Gold and Gold (1995) notice that instead of a small flow of affluent and leisured upper-class visitors coming to Scotland, there were now tour parties of middle-class visitors. The visitors were now looking for different things and places, especially areas far away, traditional, authentic and offering solitude – as Scotland was promoted in that way. The travellers journeying in pursuit of their interests were thus venturing into ever remoter parts of rural Scotland. This helped to bring the country together as a composite whole. Additionally, the affirmation of the Highlands in Scottish identity can be correlated with the sense of Scottish nationality. Bardsley (2002) believes that it was through the Highlands that the relationship between historical change and Scottish nationalism was negotiated. Scott's sentimentalisation of the Highlands, which had been subdued and depopulated by punitive actions, was important in correcting some of the distorted versions of the Scottish Highlands that came in the earlier period.

Isolated Identities in a Complex Whole

The earlier period was instrumental in creating a distinctive niche of individual destinations with their areas of speciality, which continued in later years with newer forms of travel and more developed tourism forms. The development of the automobile engine, road transport and increased car ownership took the driving seat. Private motor transport remade Scottish tourism in the 20th century. Motor touring that began in the 1920s increased in the post-war period, triggered by growing prosperity and leisure time. With motor transport there was greater mobility and control over travel plans, giving tourists the opportunity to go in search of dialogue between the modern world, and the authentic and unchanging traditions of the countryside (Gruffudd, 1994). Even the railways linked up with bus services as feeders for railway traffic. Aviation further consolidated the visitor flow and had a considerable impact on Scottish tourism. Most remarkably, it re-established links with expatriate communities, and tourists started to flock to Scotland for cultural events such as the Highland Games, ceilidhs and clan gatherings (Gold & Gold, 1995). We will see in Chapter 7 that travel to one's homeland enhances a sense of cultural affinity and can yield strong nationalistic feelings.

With all these developments tourism became more organised, and newer promotional styles were introduced. But the image of Scotland largely remained the same, resting heavily on traditional images – emphasising tradition and tartanry, sentimentality and romanticism, nostalgia and heritage (Gold & Gold, 1995). While rural Scotland continued to depict the traditional side, cities and industrial areas moved their focus to heritage and nostalgia, creating for Scots a more distinctive sense of themselves in the tourist market. This was seen prominently in the case of Scottish cities. Being embedded within the overall image of Scotland, these cities successfully created their own image through branding. McCrone (2001: 28) considers that Scotland remains a country of 'city-states' with distinctive identities and cultures. The cities of Aberdeen, Dundee, Edinburgh and Glasgow wield considerable economic and cultural pull. The competition for dominance over these pull factors can be more aggressively seen between the two rival cities of Glasgow and Edinburgh. They have both used tourism as an important tool in their regeneration and branding exercises and have successfully established themselves on the tourist map.

The most important development since the world wars has been development of a destination through branding. The perception of a place is not just about images and descriptions, it is also about enactments of being there, forms of eating and drinking there, and the branding of objects that come to represent the place (Cuthill, 2004: 59). In the last five decades tourism has been an important aspect in the branding of cities. Branding has significantly contributed to the transformation of Glasgow from its inward-looking, post-industrial slump, to a confident, outward-looking, economically regenerated destination city. Edensor (2004) believes places are continually reconstituted through the multiple flows that centre on them, and the ways in which they are sutured into more or less stable networks of mobility.

The case of Glasgow shows how the reconstitution process can develop over time. With the rise of merchant traders in the 16th and 17th centuries and rapid expansion of trade in the 18th century, Glasgow achieved the distinction of being the second city of the Empire in the 19th century. But the early stories of success took a contrasting turn due to an industrial decline of enormous proportions in the 20th century, coupled with the post-war housing crisis. The new economic base was recreated with the help of the service sector within a short period of time in the latter half of the 20th century. This was achieved through various efforts directed towards a cultural renaissance in the 1980s and 1990s. Remarkable in this was the awarding of the European City of Culture (ECoC) to Glasgow in the year 1990. This event greatly helped transform the image of the city into a unique, dynamic place, encompassing its culture as embedded in its architecture, design, engineering, shipbuilding, education, religion and sport. During the ECoC year over 3400 public events took place, involving performers and artists from 23 countries. Forty major works were commissioned in the performing and visual arts, and there were 60 world premieres in theatre and dance. In addition, there were some 3979 performances, 656 theatrical productions and 1901 exhibitions – not forgetting the 157 sporting events (www.glasgow.gov.uk). The regeneration of Glasgow has continued and tourism and other service sectors have contributed enormously to this effort.

According to VisitScotland (2013c), Glasgow attracted 2.2 million staying visits in 2011. Visits from the domestic (British) market making up 78%, some 1.73 million visits. The international market represented 22% of all visits, with 0.47 million visits. The average length of stay in Glasgow is 2.1 nights (domestic visitor) and 6.1 nights (overseas visitor). Within the British market, 55% are from England, 43% from Scotland and 2% from Wales. Averaging visitor figures over the last three years, the US is Glasgow's largest single overseas market, followed by Germany and France. According to VisitScotland (2013c), annual figures for each market can be highly variable, reflecting factors such as changing market conditions, availability of direct flights and specific events, for example sports events. Until recently, Glasgow was branding itself with the strap-line, 'Scotland with style', to further consolidate its image as a contemporary modern Scottish city.

Similarly, Edinburgh has also thrived on tourism and the service industry. It is a long-established tourist destination. It was never a centre for manufacturing industry but relied on printing and brewing in the 18th and 19th centuries. Despite its failure to become an industrial city, it remained a city of bankers and lawyers. During the entire 19th century it was flooded with various monuments. Since the 20th century tourism has contributed remarkably to the regeneration of the city. The establishment of the Edinburgh Festival in the year 1947 has been instrumental in internationalising Edinburgh, which has embedded Scottishness in its image. The growth of the heritage industry in Britain has not left Edinburgh untouched and the city has seen much new heritage added to its tourist attractions. Its heritage value has been recognised, and Edinburgh has achieved World Heritage Site status – designated to its mediaeval Old Town and Georgian New Town. Though predominantly a heritage city, Edinburgh now has more than one persona, and like any capital city it has the remit that it represents the nation as a whole. Importantly, tourism has been one of the key media used to disseminate the image of Edinburgh. For example, since 2005 Edinburgh has been branding itself with a new strap-line, 'Inspiring Capital', to represent a more cohesive image of the city with the object of promoting tourism, trade and investment. About 85% of all jobs in Edinburgh are in the service industries; it is one of Europe's prominent cities in terms of hotel occupancy (City of Edinburgh Council, 2009). The 'iconic' features of the city contribute to making a popular image of Edinburgh that is largely articulated by tourism.

According to VisitScotland (2013b), the year 2011 was very successful in terms of the number of visitors to Edinburgh. The city attracted nearly 3.7 million staying visits in 2011. Visits from the domestic market made up 64% of those staying visits, some 2.35 million visits. The international market represented 36% of all staying visits, with 1.34 million visits. This is a much higher proportion than for Scotland as a whole, which stands at 15%. The average length of stay in Edinburgh is 2.3 nights (domestic visitor) and 4.3 nights (overseas visitor), which is lower than the national average of 3.4 nights (domestic) and 7.3 nights (overseas) respectively. Within the British market, 63% of visitors are from England, 34% from Scotland and 3% from Wales. Taking visitor figures averaged over the last three years, the US is Edinburgh's largest single overseas market, followed by Germany, Ireland, France, Spain, Australia and Italy.

Producing Scotland through Regional Branding

We have seen in the earlier sections that the image of Scotland does not remain fixed: it is varied and diverse. Scotland assumed an initial image of a romantic country, which was consolidated with the diversification of the tourism product base in the later stages. However, the major thrust in terms of the tourism identity of Scotland has largely rested on the country's natural and scenic beauty, its historical legacy and heritage attractions. The continuation of this trend is still the hallmark of regional branding efforts. The existing efforts of regional tourist boards in promoting Scottish regions form the continuation of an older trend and are flooded with dominant images of Scotland.

In 2005 a new VisitScotland network came into being. The erstwhile 14 Area Tourism Boards were dissolved to be replaced by VisitScotland's area tourist offices, (i) functioning as a single point of contact for tourism businesses; and (ii) acting as one team for tourism; the network is responsible for the delivery and implementation of a national strategy complemented by local tourism action plans. These regional boards have their own marketing sections that team up with stakeholders to produce a distinctive narrative of their region. These regions have sought refuge in creating their own brand proposition which is dependent on the traditional image of Scotland. It is important to note that a traditional image of Scotland is a paradox in the context of 19th and 20th century Scotland, which was a pioneering and highly industrialised society, built around iron, coal and shipbuilding (King, 2007). However, the image of the Scottish nation is strongly embedded in its traditional representation.

Within Scotland each region has attempted to identify its own niche and is vigorously trying to establish its distinctive image on the tourist map of Scotland. This is evident from the use of separate strap-lines in these regions to establish their individual brand images. Additionally, a closer look into the regional websites of these regions gives an indication of how each one is trying to project the image of a region conterminous with the image of Scotland. The image of Scotland in the narratives of these regions presents itself through its landscape, nature, wilderness, mountains, lakes, history, tradition and culture. Some examples of these regions' diverging foci are:

> Take time to discover your perfect break now so that when you arrive you can relax and let the landscape and atmosphere of this inspiring corner of Scotland work its spell on you. (Dumfries and Galloway)

> The Isle of Arran has the best of what the rest of Scotland has to offer. A beautiful coastline with pretty villages is complemented by a rugged and

> mountainous interior in the north and green rolling hills and woodland in the south. (Ayrshire and Arran)
>
> Loch Lomond has long been immortalised in lyric verse and song. The single biggest expanse of inland water in the British Isles, Loch Lomond brings together two very different Scotlands. (Loch Lomond, Helenburgh and West Dunbartonshire)
>
> Uncover a different part of Scotland, where two thousand years of magic, mystery, and romance, are interwoven across a land as unspoiled as it is rich in history, tradition and culture. Whatever your reason for visiting Scotland, explore for yourself the legacy of ancient peoples, kings and queens, adventurers and inventors. (Angus and Dundee)
>
> Expect a warm welcome as locals and visitors alike enjoy the best of our rich heritage and culture including spectacular street theatre, music, storytelling, and of course our world famous ceilidhs. (Highlands)
>
> Take the opportunity to experience our unique culture, hospitality and absolute freedom – now there's no excuse! (Hebrides)

Two important observations can be made of the above narratives: (i) the majority of the regions overwhelmingly rely on a popular imagining of Scotland created through Scottish wilderness, nature and landscape to promote the region; (ii) regions rely less on local distinctiveness but more on images which are tied strongly to Scottish heritage and which are part of Scotland's self-identity.

Scholars have argued that geography has often acted as a tool for clarifying and fostering a sense of national identity (see Hooson, 1994). Landscape assumes special significance as countries commonly depict themselves in landscape terms: for instance, every national anthem praises special scenic splendours or nature's unique bounties (Lowenthal, 1994). What we see in the tourism efforts of Scotland is that all of the regions rely on the Scottish landscape. The regions are principally relying on nature to project their distinctiveness and specifically focus on valleys and glens and other aspects of landscape. This is important because, as Cosgrove (1994) points out, both Welsh and Scottish nationalisms have constructed their own meaning from mountain landscapes, valleys and glens, drawing as heavily on the natural world as upon their separate languages to construct differences from England. The image of Scotland produced through regional tourism brands is conterminous with the nationalist narrative, in other words it bolsters the cultural sense of being Scottish.

Some regions have tried to focus on their heritage rather than on nature and landscape alone. The case of Stirling shows a conspicuous stress on Scotland's militaristic tradition. 'It is here that Scotland's historic past and exciting future are both very much in evidence', says its website. A sense of militarism is strongly tied to Scottish nationalism. The focus on Scottish militaristic heritage in the promotion of tourism is an assertion of nationalism that is well recognised (Edensor, 1997a). The Stirling website says: 'It was here that William Wallace – the Braveheart – and Robert the Bruce won independence for Scotland. In memorial was built the William Wallace Monument, while Bruce's historic victory is vividly remembered at the Bannockburn Heritage Centre.' It must be noted that some commentators opine that the place identity of Stirling is largely manufactured by tourism, with the help of a nationalist discourse (Aitchison, 1999). Much of this has happened because of the legacy of William Wallace, Robert the Bruce and others, showcased to tourists as attractions in and around Stirling.

Edinburgh and Lothian promotes the already existing image of festivals which Edinburgh has so famously established.

> The beautiful city of Edinburgh is an enchanting place for a spring and summer break. With a wonderful menu of events and festivals including the spring International Science Festival, the Film Festival and the summer Festivals including the Jazz, Book and Fringe – you'll be spoilt for choice.

Whereas Aberdeen mentions its industrial heritage, but places strong emphasis on its nature, coastline and history:

> Home to the country's largest national park, a dramatically imposing coastline and of course the city itself, there is so much to explore in Aberdeen City and Shire. Fusing striking granite architecture, a rich and inspiring history, a dynamic modern arts scene and perhaps Scotland's strongest industrial heritage; the country's third largest city offers a host of treasures, just waiting to be explored again & again.

We see that regional tourism boards rely heavily on the traditional image of Scotland that stresses its landscape and nature at its core. Heritage forms another important part in creating a sense of Scotland. We have noted earlier that both landscape and heritage are important elements of Scottish identity, strongly epitomising Scotland as a nation.

Conclusions

This chapter has shown how identity has always been part and parcel of Scottish tourism. The travel accounts of early writers were instrumental in creating an image of Scotland as a nation. Tourism activities that in later years became more diversified across wider areas and various other regions and images started to form complementary images of the country. Further developed, tourism is now projecting a diverse yet composite image of Scotland. The contemporary image of the country is still the one that has been created and reinforced for over two centuries and that still forms a popular image of Scotland. This has resulted in a highly skewed imagery of Scotland in favour of one region and cultural identity, and there is a gap between the touristic image and the social reality of the country. Tourism has remained an important tool for creating and projecting this image and for outsiders it is these images which are popular identifiers of the Scottish nation.

What Glasgow and Edinburgh show us is that tourism has been the principal medium through which the image of these cities has either been formed or is being recreated. Yet both essentially also carry an image of being distinctively Scottish cities. The trend is also visible in the promotional efforts of regional tourism boards. The various regions of Scotland have been trying to create their own distinctive brand image. The image they are relying on in promoting themselves through branding is the one created and reinforced for over two centuries. The reliance upon this long-established image gives two distinct advantages to Scotland. First, it has a comparative advantage in marketing terms, and second, it helps in bolstering an authentic sense of Scotland. This fits perfectly with VisitScotland's plan. VisitScotland has identified the future of Scottish tourism to be focused on the concept of authenticity (Future Foundation & VisitScotland, 2005, cited in Yeoman *et al.*, 2007). I have argued earlier that a sense of authenticity is a strong manifestation of identity because it helps position oneself as the 'other'. King (2007) makes the point that linking authenticity to tourism in Scotland is a political process, as Scotland is an identity-seeking nation. We have seen in earlier chapters that seeking identity in Scotland is strongly embedded in its sense of nationalism.

The popular image of Scotland rests on the images created by tourism. The early travel accounts helped create this perception, but the diversification and growth of tourism has intensely popularised this. The prominence of the Scottish Highlands in tourism contributed to establishing the Highlands and its features, such as lochs and mountains, as an identifier of Scotland. This mostly happened during the second phase, as outlined earlier, when the growth of Scottish tourism mostly revolved around the Highlands, though there were a couple of attractions in the Lowlands. Recent developments show tourism is widespread across the country, but the images the tourism industry chooses to portray are more limited and are focused on those traditional ones that place the Highlands and natural landscapes at their centre.

What is evident from these observations is that Scottish identity is steeped in the landscape of the past. This indicates the very important role of heritage tourism in Scotland. What we see from some of the regional tourism efforts is that heritage is used more positively for the promotion of tourism. All the regions make claims to Scottish identity through their cultural or natural association with the popular image of Scotland. Cities like Edinburgh and Glasgow are heavily reliant on their heritage. Heritage tourism is considered a carrier of identity (Timothy & Boyd, 2003), and, as we have noted in Chapter 2, it acts as a mechanism of dissemination for nationalism and other ideologically loaded discourses (Graham *et al.*, 2000). In the next chapter we will look at how the heritage resources of Edinburgh are interpreted by the tour guides on the Edinburgh tour buses to narrate the story of the Scottish nation.

4 'Narrating' the Scottish Nation on Tour Buses

Introduction

In this chapter I draw on the role of tour guides as 'mediators' of local culture to show how they exemplify the idea of the Scottish nation and nationhood during their work on the Edinburgh tour bus. Guides' interpretation of Edinburgh on the tour covers wide-ranging issues that bear immense significance to contemporary Scotland. The reading of their interpretation and their emphasis on Scottish distinctiveness is informed by a broader 'national' discourse in Scotland that is marked by an increased nationalist sentiment. Their tour narratives give us a deeper insight into Scotland and its ancient nationhood, military prowess and strong culture, Scottish devolution and its future aspirations. These narratives are not apolitical or unopinionated and they 'mediate' the Scottish nation in such a way that exalts its 'national' existence. I argue that the guides' narrative is an expression of nationalism, and tour guides are in one form 'nationalists', who assemble various artefacts and historical resources, exemplify the Scottish nation and stimulate their sense of Scottish national identity and nationalism.

My purpose is to see how guides utilise history, myths, symbols and traditions to construct a gaze, and to study their account of Edinburgh to ascertain whether it corresponds to the idea of Scottish nationhood. I will look into the sites, aspects and the story that is selected, emphasised and interpreted by the tour guides on the tour. The study is informed by the observation that the stories and narratives of the tour bus guides can be a window through which to glimpse the socio-cultural undercurrent of Scottish society and identity because the guides' accounts are based on their country's socio-cultural, historical, political and economic contexts or situation (e.g. Ap & Wong, 2001).

Scholars have made a good case for tourism by emphasising the non-material importance that the activity of tourism incorporates. While theorising tourism as a 'gaze', Urry (2002) makes the point that there is a social and physical relation between the *gazer* (the tourist) and the object of the *gaze* in the organisation of which guides, together with other professionals, play a significant role. This relation has been referred to by some scholars as 'mediator', 'interpreter', 'leader', 'information-giver' and so on (Cohen, 1985b; Dahles, 2002; Holloway, 1981). Guides are essentially managers of this relationship, who use various attractions and artefacts as a medium to communicate between the two sides. Drawing on the gastronomic theory of nation, I contend in this chapter that the language of this communication is in many ways close to the ideals of 'nationalists'.

The gastronomic theory of nation views nations as being composed of discrete elements, with their cultures possessing a variety of ingredients. For example, Scottish identity was shaped by various influences in the past: for instance, Gaelic kingship, the Reformation, the Enlightenment, James Macpherson, tartan, whisky, bagpipes, Culloden, Bannockburn, Edinburgh Castle, Robert Burns, Sir Walter Scott, Robert the Bruce and so on. According to gastronomic theory, nationalists and their followers put together the various ingredients of the nation – history, symbols, myths and languages – in much the same way as 'pub owners put together the ploughman's lunch' (Smith, 1995: 2). Smith (1995) says that the modern nation is a composite artefact, put together from a rich variety of cultural sources in which nationalists act as archaeologists, whose activity consists of the rediscovery and reinterpretation of their historic past. I will show in this chapter that by selecting and presenting various artefacts, histories, symbols, myths and interpretations, guides assemble the nation, in the same way the 'nationalists' do, in the regeneration of their national community.

The Role of Tour Guiding

The role of the tour guide in the tourist experience is well-articulated by scholars (Dahles, 2002; Holloway, 1981; Macdonald, 2006). Scholars have shown that guides play an important role in cultural tourism in selecting, glossing and interpreting signs (Bowman, 1992; Cohen, 1985b; Holloway, 1981; Schimidt, 1979). Importantly, guides translate 'the strangeness of a foreign culture into a cultural idiom familiar to the visitors' (Cohen, 1985b: 15). Cohen notes that guides provide not only access to an otherwise non-public territory, but they also serve as a 'mentor, as a guru to the novice, adept, or seeker, guiding him towards insight, enlightenment or any other exalted spiritual state' (1985: 10). In other words, guides facilitate access and try to integrate what is seen into a coherent and meaningful image of a place (Dahles, 2002).

The significance of the guide as an intermediary or facilitator has been recognised by anthropologists who refer to them as 'cultural brokers'. Though not specifying guides, these 'cultural brokers' are those who emerge to manage relations between 'hosts' and 'guests' (Smith, 1989). The latest addition to the list of anthropologists is Salazar (2010), who argues that guides have assumed the role of ambassador of local culture and tradition. He shows us that guides rely on a wide range of sources and attributes to structure their narratives, and this contributes to the inflow of foreign tourism imaginaries and discourses. He explains that through these attributes tour guides process their discourses in a way that presents the local scene as paradise and that the representation of their own culture and heritage is deeply rooted in ideological imaginaries of 'otherness'.

Guides play multiple roles and 'initiate the tourists into the culture of the host country' (Holloway, 1981: 387). In this process, interpretation assumes a key place. Through the interpretive tools they have, guides mobilise heritage properties and objects to demonstrate the past to visitors, which increases their understanding and appreciation of the resources presented to them (Dewar, 1989). The interpretive presentation of guides is not limited to a simple description of historic events and people, it also inspires a feeling for a moment of history (Craig, 1989: 108). Tilden (1977) prominently expresses this role in his guiding principles of interpretation. He recognises that a careful interpretation should relate properly to the visitor, be inspiring, be communicative and provocative, be holistic and should apply no single or uniform approach.

By providing interpretation, tour guides help enhance the destination satisfaction and facilitate in encapsulating the essence of a place. They provide a window onto a site, region or country (Pont, 1993). Holloway (1981) argues that as interpreters of the host country, guides simultaneously find themselves acting as ambassadors for their country, and that they may personify many of the national characteristics of the host population for overseas tourists who may have little direct contact with the indigenous population. This role of the guide is also captured by Del Casino and Hanna (2000), who argue that tourism workers are so much part of the performance of a site that they, in a sense, 'become' it.

The role of the tourist guide is looked at in greater detail by Cohen (1985b, 2004). He analyses the transition of the role of the guide under a broader conceptualisation which sees the tour guide as a leader and as a mediator. In an institutionalised tourism system the role of the guide increases from mere selection of sights and information to more sophisticated interpretation. However, this interpretation cannot be guaranteed an authentic one. Cohen notes that depending on the nature of the tourism product, the guides sometimes might 'fabricate' the story at a tourist attraction, particularly if the attraction is 'staged' for tourists. Despite this, guides do not lose their important role as a mediator who acts as an intermediary between cultures, because in executing their duties the principal expectation of guides from the mass of tourists is that they provide information and interpretation of the sites visited (Nettekoven, 1979, cited in Cohen, 2004), and tourists very rarely question the authenticity of the facts presented. This increases the significance of guides in the process of site sacralisation, which according to MacCannell (1999) involves five stages: naming, framing and elevation, enshrinement, mechanical reproduction and social reproduction.

In this context, Gurung *et al.*'s (1996) idea concerning the guide's role is relevant. They make a distinction between the two roles of tour guide – as tour manager and experience manager – both of which are important in the site sacralisation process. The guide's task involves the organisation of the itinerary and the selection and interpretation of sites in an interactive process with tourists. This suggests that guides play a pivotal role in influencing 'the visitor's' impression and attitudes, as well as enhancing their appreciation and understanding of their surroundings. But how much freedom they enjoy in narrating the tour depends on the nature of power relations within which they have to operate – an area very few scholars have looked into.

Dahles (2002) notes that studies on the political role of tour guiding are lacking. He objects to the overemphasis on the role of the guide as a mediator, who is portrayed as 'someone who builds bridges among different groups of people' (Dahles, 2002: 784) through the deployment of money, services, access, and information (Gurung *et al.*, 1996). Dahles (2002) challenges the naivety with which the role of tour guides is understood and maintains that 'the process of mediation is not as innocent and unproblematic as this perspective implies'. He argues that guiding is essentially political in nature and there is a power relationship within which guides operate. Macdonald (2006), who has shown that mediation is not an apolitical process, further illustrates this idea. She suggests that tour guides are engaged in encoding a 'preferred reading' to the visitors and conveying a particular account. According to her, any attempt to encode meaning is shaped by the conventions of the medium and genre, audiences, and the materialities of the tour context. However, she misses an important point here that the encoding of meaning by guides is strongly informed by a country's socio-cultural background and the 'national' context in which they operate.

Dahles (2002) has shown that in Indonesia the guide's role as a mediator is largely determined by the political landscape of the country. He reports that the Indonesian government uses tourism strategically to address or promote issues of national significance and develop a desired national identity. The 'formal guides' are trained by the government to provide politically and ideologically correct narratives. Another example of the deployment of guides by governments has also been noted by Reisinger and Steiner (2006), who argue that guided tours can be an effective instrument for governments to control tourists and their contacts with the host society and to disseminate images and information preferred by the authorities.

Whilst acknowledging the political role tour guides can play, I do not subscribe to the idea that all governments necessarily have a role in producing such a political narrative. Instead, guides may be self-censored on many occasions and their narration is more an outcome of their personal experience or feelings than any forced political orientation. Jorgensen (2003), who has looked into the role of guides in the construction of Irish identity on board County Wicklow tour buses in Ireland, finds that guides are independent and have more control over what is to be included and omitted. He believes tourists' interpretation of Irish identity is negotiated and influenced by their own socio-cultural position, irrespective of whether the government intervenes or not. In the following paragraphs, we will see that the narrative of the tour guide in Edinburgh is greatly informed by the socio-political context of Scotland. Guides constantly remind visitors of Scotland's nationhood and nationalism through the mentioning of the devolution of parliament and other historical resources that assert Scottish distinctiveness.

Why Edinburgh?

There are distinctive reasons to choose Edinburgh. First, Edinburgh is Scotland's capital city. Capital cities have remained one of the foremost tourist attractions. In many instances they serve as the first port of call to international tourists, and as a centre for business, education, arts and politics they draw domestic visitors in great numbers. In addition, capital cities are also significant for tourism because of their cultural, heritage and symbolic roles (C.M. Hall, 2002). Capital cities offer a vantage point for understanding a nation, since they frequently host major national and cultural institutions. They also play a wider role in the portrayal, preservation and promotion of national heritage and for showcasing national culture (Therborn, 1996). If the capital city is itself a top-class heritage attraction, as Edinburgh is, there is an even greater interest in it. Roche (2000) believes that tourism can represent a pilgrimage to a sacred centre, often through a capital city which is the most appropriate representation of the country (cited in Urry, 2002). Edinburgh assumes such a distinction of being a 'sacred-centre'.

A second reason for choosing Edinburgh is that tourist attractions in Edinburgh are dominated by historical resources. Edinburgh is home to monuments, museums, archaeological sites, and other cultural resources for which a significant part of the city is listed as a World Heritage Site. These resources are also a means of affirming and reinforcing national identities for tourists as well as citizens (Lanfant *et al.*, 1995; McLean, 1998). Additionally, Edinburgh hosts various events and festivals which are in many other instances used by countries to unify and manage their new national populace. Many countries have employed special events and festivals to recreate culture, manufacture nationhood, national identity and patriotism and even develop xenophobia and public disdain towards other ethnicities (Graham, 1996; Hall & McArthur, 1996). But most significantly, Edinburgh sits on so many heritage and historical resources that it stands to represent the existing social and political values and structures of Scotland. Timothy and Boyd (2003) believe that it is not uncommon for presiding governments to utilise heritage in one form or another to shape public opinion, to build nationalism and to create images that reflect their political ideals. Thus, the story constructed by the guides, I believe, is in effect framing an idea of the Scottish nation to visitors.

Data for this chapter were collected through participant observation on the city tour buses in Edinburgh. I undertook a covert observation to minimise any bias that might result from the presence of the researcher interacting and possibly changing the very nature of social relationships in the setting. However, prior consent was obtained from the guides and the tour bus company. Once the guides consented, I took the bus tour at different times, not necessarily informing the guide every time I boarded the tour bus. The guides were informed that the purpose of doing this was to study their narrative without it being noticed that someone was studying them. I checked with guides that they were happy about doing this, and this was established, which allowed me to remain a covert observer. A drawback of being a complete observer sometimes is that it does not allow the researcher to clarify meanings and ask questions concerning things that are not readily understood by the researcher (Hesse-Biber & Leavy, 2006). In order to avoid such cases, I interviewed tour guides at different times, at their convenience. At the end of the bus tour sessions informal short interviews were carried out with 15 guides, noting that not all guides were prepared to enter into discussion with the researcher. Additionally, some guides had to start consecutive tours on other buses while others had a very brief interval between their tours, reducing the amount of time available for interview. This being the case, some of the interviews were undertaken during the lunch tours and not immediately after each tour.

Assembling the Scottish Nation

Narratives of tour guides on the tour buses are varied. 'Our tours cover all aspects of Edinburgh's history and culture and give our passengers a comprehensive insight into all aspects of life in Edinburgh now and throughout history. There is no central theme' says Elaine Green, Sales Manager at the bus tours (personal communication, 2008). However, there is greater focus on various clusters of Scottish heritage, for instance, Scottish history, culture and city architecture in Edinburgh. All the tour buses run through the common core area of the city, marking historical monuments, though with different routes.

All tours start from Waverley railway station. On the other side stands Scotland's tallest monumental tower, built in honour of Sir Walter Scott – the creator of the Waverley novels, from whom the station gets its name. As noted in an earlier chapter, Sir Walter Scott made the biggest contribution to the formation of Scottish national identity. One guide notes, 'Sir Walter Scott is a famous author whose monument you can notice on the left – huge Gothic monument – 200 feet high, 287 steps to the top. And it's the greatest monument that was designed for an author.'

The Edinburgh tour bus fulfils all three of the distinctive roles of heritage assigned by Meethan (2001), that is, it is an economic resource, has a political role, and is a marker of identity. Its economic role is well emphasised, as it is the second highest paid attraction in Edinburgh and received 511,421 visitors in 2012 (VisitScotland, 2013a). My interest here is in the prominence of the second and third roles, where guides' efforts are directed towards introducing Scottish heritage to visitors. It is clearly visible from the tour guides' narratives that Scotland's distinctive identity features most prominently in the tour. Smith (1991) believes that nation and national identity must be seen as a creation of nationalism and its proponents, and their significance and celebration are the handiwork of nationalists. Since there is very little distinction between nation and national identity, it can be construed that these identity markers are in effect an act of showcasing nationalism. The guides' narration during the tour assembles the various resources of Scottish nationhood that can be studied, grouped under the following four themes: the Scottish Parliament, distinctiveness from England, Scotland's ancient nationhood and Scottish militarism.

The Scottish Parliament

The Scottish Parliament is mentioned prominently throughout the entire tour. This is contrary to the fact that Edinburgh Castle remains Scotland's largest tourist attraction. Guides give the Scottish Parliament a meticulous description, greater than that of the castle. Though the latest statistics on visitor numbers are not available, the parliament was at one point the seventh highest paid attraction in Scotland; its visitor centre received more than 350,000 visitors in 2007 (VisitScotland, 2008).

While the permanent building at Holyrood was being constructed, the parliament was temporarily seated in the General Assembly Hall of the Church of Scotland on the Royal Mile in Edinburgh. The General Assembly Hall is a part of the School of Divinity of the University of Edinburgh. On approaching Edinburgh Castle a guide points out an insignificant building in front of the castle, noting, 'this to your right is New College, the University's Theology department, which was a temporary home to the Scottish Parliament until 2001'.

The escalating costs of the construction of the new parliament building have remained one of the biggest controversies in Scotland and a subject of widespread criticism. In 1997 the White Paper estimated that a new building would have a net construction cost of £40 million, which was based on the presumption that the old Royal High School building, since renamed 'New Parliament House', would be used. All guides mention that the Royal High School building had initially been planned for the parliament. They show visitors the signage 'New Parliament House' written in the street leading to the school. But after the devolution referendum it was quickly announced that the high school was inadequate for the parliament, and negotiations began for a new building on a new site. The Spanish architect Enric Miralles designed the building that was initially costed at £109 million, which was before a major increase in space was made. However, the estimated final cost reached £431 million. The Scottish Parliament building opened for business on the 7 September 2004.

The funding disaster, the architectural details and what happens in the Chambers are thoroughly explained. A guide says 'The building coming up on your right should have cost £40 million, but it was completed for £431 million. Just a little bit over budget, the Scottish Parliament.' One guide begins with the architectural description of the parliament,

> Our Scottish Parliament on your right was designed by Spanish architect the late Enric Miralles. It is modern. The Parliament was officially opened by the Queen in 2004. As you go down right they have a visitor centre with all the information – the history of the Parliament, what they do and a nice café and a good shop. And it's lovely inside. A lot of people feel the Parliament has a Spanish look similar to the work of Gaudi at Barcelona. Miralles the architect was from Barcelona.

Another guide offers an invitation to see Scotland's own functioning democracy, asking visitors to take the guided tour offered by the parliament, most preferably to see Thursday morning's question hour with the first minister. She makes the following remarks on Scottish democratic culture within the parliamentary building:

> The debating chamber in the Scottish parliament looks nothing like the debating chamber in Westminster where people are face to face; where the distance between the two sides is too short to stop people from fighting. The debating chamber in the Scottish parliament is semi-circular, resembling very much the debating chamber of the European Parliament: this is to promote collaboration and debate. And something more interesting is that there are more seats for the public than the MSPs (Member of Scottish Parliament).

The above comments by the guide mark Scotland's distinctiveness from that of the Union of Great Britain or England, and instead bring Scotland closer to Europe. Hearn (2000) has noted that the conceptual connections between Scottishness and being British and its Protestant appeal have weakened over the 20th century, while those between Scottishness and socialism and Europeanness have become stronger. The above example confirms this. A similar case was seen in the regeneration of Glasgow, wherein Glasgow adopted a 'European' theme in its 'place marketing' tool. Bianchini and Schwengel (2001) attribute this to the parallel and related resurgence of Scottish nationalism and Europeanism.

The feeling of closeness to Europeanism and European integration in relation to the rise of Scottish nationalism is not new, as some commentators have noted. Ichijo (2004) argues that Scottish nationalism differs to that of English nationalism in the very issue of attitude towards the European Union, of which Scotland is an ardent supporter and England less so. Reference here must be made to the Scottish Nationalist Party, which in 1988 made a U-turn in its approach to the European Union by adopting 'Independence in Europe'. According to Ichijo (2003), Europe is a convenient point of reference for the Scots to assert their uniqueness and, in this context, their pro-European past is effective in maintaining a Scottish identity and their own understanding of the world.

In describing the parliament, a pre-recorded tour guide (voice) explains Scottish devolution, its statutory role and power to raise tax. It says the parliament does not have tax-raising powers, but has tax-varying power, which has not yet been used. The full power it has in deciding health and education policies in Scotland is mentioned. These descriptions give visitors an idea of the constitutional status of Scotland within the Union.

Scotland had an independent parliament with a legislature known as the Three Estates before the Act of Union in 1707. Initial Scottish proposals in the negotiation over the Union suggested a devolved parliament be retained in Scotland, which was not finally agreed upon. For the next 300 years the lack of a Scottish Parliament has remained an important element in Scottish national identity. Parliament in Scotland is a strictly nationalist project: first, it reinforces national identity precisely because it pursues a policy agenda in which it is likely to find the division of powers (McCrone, 2001); second, the term nationalism in Scotland, according to Hearn (2000), must be understood broadly to include both the demand for full independence and the more limited – now realised – demand for a devolved parliament within the United Kingdom framework. One guide mentions this devolution,

> On the right is Parliament. In 1999, our government devolved and Scotland got its Parliament. This building was inaugurated in 2004, it cost a lot more than it should have... and it opened later than it should have opened. But it has won five architecture awards and was declared building of the year in 2001. And if you take a guided tour you realise how lovely a masterpiece it really is.

The prominence of the parliament in the tour is very important to note, as Smith (1991) believes that a nationalist language and symbolism is broader than an ideology or ideological movements: it often connects that ideology with the 'mass sentiments' or wider segments of the designated population, notably through slogans, ideas, symbols and ceremonies. At the same time, nationalist language and symbolism span both the cognitive and expressive dimensions, linking up with broader aspirations and feelings among both elites and wider strata. According to Smith, notions of autonomy and authenticity and symbols of self-reliance and of national community – for example, re-enactments of resistance events, or symbols of landscape and historical monuments, or local products, crafts or sports – exemplify the fusion of cognitive and expressive aspects and the links with wider sentiments and aspirations.

The politics of the English–Scottish divide

As Thomas Eriksen put it: 'We are not only because we have something in common, but perhaps chiefly because we are not them' (2004: 57). For Scotland, this 'them' is England. Scotland's nationalism to some extent thrives on opposition to or (anti)Englishness. Squires (undated) argues that it was the Scots' relationship with the English that gave birth to ardent

Scottish nationalism. It would be inappropriate to reduce Scottish nationalism to a reactionary anti-Englishness, but scholars agree that Englishness undoubtedly plays a role in relation to Scottishness, a role arising out of a long and complex history of rivalry and interdependence (Hearn, 2000; Hobsbawm, 1983, 1999). A study by ESRC (2005) on Scottish devolution showed that Anglophobia runs at an average of 38% amongst Scots. According to Hearn (2000), Scots are used to living in the cultural shadow of England, having their history, language and culture measured against an English standard. He believes Scottish culture has tended to be crudely stereotyped, portrayed as quaint and romantic, a pastiche of kilts, clans and bagpipes, and somehow suspended in a distant past, no longer truly relevant. He adds that these images and attitudes have been created as much by the Scots, especially expatriates and the middle class, as by the English. But the result nonetheless has been resentment. He notes that many Scots believe that greater control over their own politics would foster a more confident and self-assured cultural identity (Nairn, 1997). There are numerous examples of this complex and the strong sense of identity.

An example of resentment against England on the tour is seen from a guide who introduces a flat where the author Defoe lived during the early days of the Union. She introduces Defoe as an English spy, sent to report what people thought about the union of the parliaments in 1707. She gives her opinion, that 'people did not fancy being governed from more than 400 miles away'. This also shows that the guide's interpretation of historical fact is further shaped by the reality of contemporary politics.

The tour guides construct a divide between English and Scottish wherever such a distinction can be made. A bus tour covers Charlotte Square, which contains the official residence of Scotland's first minister. Upon reaching the residence a guide narrates:

> In England we have three main political parties: the Conservatives, Liberal Democrats and Labour. In Scotland we have four and the fourth one is the Scottish Nationalist Party. And they are currently in power. And the head of the Scottish Nationalist Party is Alex Salmond, our First Minister.

This introduction of a Scottish Nationalist Party (SNP) is important because it is the Nationalist Party that is advocating for complete separation from the Union and total independence.

Another guide introduces the same place in the following way:

> This is Charlotte Square. The number six Charlotte Square is the official residence of our First Minister Alex Salmond. So, number six Charlotte Square is the Scottish equivalent to 10 Downing Street in London.

A third guide makes the following remarks:

> So this is the second square of the original New Town. This is Charlotte Square. Originally to be called St George's Square because the first one was St Andrews the Scottish saint, this was to be called St Georges (after) the English saint. But they already had St Georges Square up on the university area of the city so this one is changed to Charlotte Square.

A similar distinction with England is made while introducing the Dynamic Earth attraction, which is a place for 'edutainment'. This attraction was made to celebrate the new millennium. One guide remarks, 'Our Dynamic Earth is an answer to the Millennium Dome in England.'

At another point a guide says,

> The Royal Mile is said so because it is approximately a mile long from the bottom of the royal residence right up through the Castle which is also another royal residence. I say approximately a mile because it is a mile and a hundred and six yards in length. And that's the difference between a Scottish and an English mile.

Another example of the English versus Scots distinction can be seen in the bus itself. Before the start of the tour a female guide enquires as to the home nation of the visitors. There are no English visitors until she comes to the last person and finds someone English. She exclaims, 'At least we have some English here.' Upon reaching St Andrews Square the guide says, 'This is St Andrews Square, named after the patron saint of Scotland. St Andrew is what St George is for England.' During the tour, one of the tourists in the open-top bus loses her money in a gust of wind. The guide asks another tourist who helps her collect her money, 'Is it English money? It is not worth anything.' Banknotes are unique to Scotland. Despite being a part of the United Kingdom, Scotland maintains its own currency notes, unusually, issued by retail banks. Scottish banknotes carry the images of various cultural icons of Scotland, and, as has been mentioned in Chapter 2, its banknotes have at times acted as a strong defender of Scotland's distinctiveness and identity.

The complementarity between the two countries is also mentioned. While showing the big building of the Bank of Scotland, a guide says, 'It is interesting that the Bank of Scotland was established by an Englishman and the Bank of England was established by a Scotsman.' In another guide's narration the remark is made, 'now the building with a green dome, that is the Bank of Scotland, and that was started in 1695 by an Englishman the year before that the Bank of England was started by a Scotsman.' Though it conveys the integration between the two people it is also powerfully significant that they tell visitors that being Scottish is not what being English is. It must be borne in mind that many visitors from outside of Europe would have less knowledge of the cultural geography of the Union and may understand the United Kingdom itself as a cultural whole.

What we can construe from the above examples is that there is certainly a divide with England in Scotland. For a long time scholars have argued that anti-English sentiment, whether avowed or unconscious, is real and unmistakable in the Scottish populace, and it is fanned by loose talk about English indifference to Scottish sufferings and the 'English-controlled' political parties (Pryde, 1935). But, more recently, some scholars have taken the view that Scottish identity should not be looked upon as being in opposition to England. For example Bechhofer and McCrone (2009: 65) term it as 'vis-à-vis'. According to them, 'against' implies being opposed to, and that is too strong: instead they state that Scots define themselves vis-à-vis the English. It would be wise to comprehend that Scots view their identity in relation to England.

Ancient Scottish nationhood

Scotland's nationhood is a prominent feature within all the tours. One tour guide starts her tour with, 'Well this is Princes Street. The main ... (inaudible) ... in Edinburgh. Edinburgh ... the capital of Scotland. Scotland ... a nation in its own right'. She makes frequent mention of the Scottish Crown throughout her tour. She gives the following description of Edinburgh Castle at the beginning of the tour. 'In the castle you can view the Scottish Crown first worn by Robert the Bruce beside the Stone of Destiny. Until recently the latter was housed in Westminster Abbey, now returned to Edinburgh.' Another guide describes St Giles Cathedral thus, 'This is St Giles Cathedral. Some say based on the Scottish crown. Others say not.' Another guide notes, 'you can see the Church of St Giles. He is the patron saint of Edinburgh. The (inaudible) ... of Scottish crown.' All of these descriptions assert the fact of Scotland's nationhood before the Union. It must be recalled here that Scotland's nationalism has most ardently relied on figures and features of the past, mostly residing in the pre-Union era. Scottish nationhood is repeated when a description of Canongate Church is made. A guide introduces the church as follows,

> This is where Her Majesty the Queen comes to worship when she comes to Scotland. Her Majesty the Queen is not head of the Church in Scotland and so when she comes to worship she sits among the congregation.

This is an important assertion of the historical continuity of Scotland as a nation. This is also seen in the case of the castle, where another guide introduces it in this way, 'the Castle is also the home of the Scottish Crown... which is the oldest in Europe. And it is in the Crown wing of the Castle alongside the Stone of Destiny.' The continuity of an acceptable past is the principal object for any nationalist. This is manifested by a guide who says, 'The land on the other side of the river, we call Fife nowadays. Officially it is the Kingdom of Fife, because the Kings and Queens of Scotland used to live on the other side of the river.'

There is no denial of the fact that Edinburgh Castle stands as the most potent symbol of Scottish nationhood. It is also a top tourist attraction for Scotland. 'The Castle well is the top tourist attraction here in Edinburgh.' says a guide. The bus tour principally revolves around the castle. Spanning an hour, the tour allocates 40–45 minutes to the Old Town, compared to 15–20 minutes to the New Town. The castle, along with some other heritage attractions, lies in the Old Town. Upon arriving in the castle all guides make an important announcement: 'we are at the Castle now', and prescribe an allocation of two hours for visitors to explore the castle.

The guides' view of Scotland's medieval nationhood is reflected in the following,

> Coming up to the left is Rose Murray House. That's where J.K. Rowling came to become a teacher before she became a novelist. It's also where the Act of Union was signed in 1707. The Act of Union is really important because that was where Scotland lost its Parliament until 1999 when our government devolved and we got our Parliament again.

At another point another guide adds, 'Scottish law is Roman law, English law is Common Law. When we joined parliaments in 1707 we kept our own laws.' The narratives produced by guides strongly try to stress Scotland's national status before the Union, when Scotland was an independent nation.

Scottish militarism

We mentioned earlier that under certain conditions identity becomes more prominent (Lanfant, 1995a, 1995b). Certain sentiments and periods are more potent in instigating a sense of belonging. According to Ashworth (1991), war is a potent force that plays an important role in arousing powerful nationalist emotions. This is why many countries emphasise war heritage, including battlefields, national cemeteries, tombs of unknown soldiers and so on, to engender a sense of collective patriotism. Monuments represent certain sentiments under which a nation is remembered. This remembrance is retold every day by tourist guides, affirming Scotland's national ethos.

The martial tradition has long been an important part of the Scottish identity (Devine, 1994). Some scholars consider that in Scotland militarism is tied in with the idea of nationalism. Aitchison (1999: 69) looked into Stirling's heritage and concludes that,

> The iconography of nationalism is inseparable from that of militarism in the representation of Stirling's heritage. Wallace and Bruce are seen as national heroes because of their military victories. Stirling Castle and its regimental museum is a tourist attraction largely because of its militaristic heritage.

This observation remains valid in the case of Edinburgh. The castle is an excellent example which captures the country in its entirety. The castle has been a parade ground and army headquarters, and is now the most potent symbol of power and place (McCrone *et al.*, 1995). The castle is also the site of a Scottish war memorial. All the guides explain Edinburgh Castle and its entire militaristic heritage in detail during the tour. A guide comments, 'The big building up in the Castle is the barrack, the Victorian one', describing a distant view of the castle. Upon reaching the castle another guide mentions,

> The statue on either side of the Castle entrance, ... that's Robert the Bruce and William Wallace. Bruce and Wallace ... they are known as the guardians of Scotland. Famous since the film *Braveheart* 1996 with Mel Gibson. And 'Braveheart' did a wee bit more to Hollywood than Holyrood. A nice film. It did a lot for William Wallace.

Another guide also mentions the film *Braveheart*, which made the story of Robert the Bruce famous all over the world, but still believes the film to be superficial.

There are a lot of commemorative monuments to war veterans, all of which receive attention from the guides and tourists on the tour. A guide declares, 'now we are in Princes Street and ... ahead of the bus up on Calton Hill is the Nelson monument. It (inaudible) ... to represent an inverted telescope and it's there to commemorate the victory of Admiral Lord Nelson at Trafalgar against the French.' The description of war memorials sends a strong nationalistic message, which the following account of a guide makes clear, 'This is the difficult path in the tour because we are entering a lot of commemorations of the victory of British against the French and I am a French citizen in the past.' While remaining in the bus waiting for passengers at the castle a guide describes a statue, 'the chap on the horse is Douglas Haig the commander of the 1st World War. His American cousin Alexander Haig was the secretary of State under Nixon.'

What we can see from the above narratives of tour guides is that there are constant reminders that Scotland is a separate nation. The bus tour is comparable to a museum visit, where the whole city becomes a series of artefacts and guides provide the interpretation. MacCannell (1999) believes symbols of the past are collected in museums when they are small enough and when they are too large they are left outside in parks and called monuments. The abundance of monuments and architectural heritage in Edinburgh makes the city an open museum. Through the tour guides' narrative, visitors read these monuments and interpret these 'symbols of the past'. Their reading of the symbols relies on the mediatory role guides play. Guides not only mediate between the two different cultures, but, through the meaningful interpretation of historical resources, they also essentially mediate between the Scottish past and the present: the visitors imbibe 'the history' the guides present to them. Dahles (1996) has explored the way in which cultural interpreters develop the discourses on Amsterdam. He concludes that guides can construct a regular, meaningful and profitable tourist gaze. It was noticed in this study that during entire bus tours none of the visitors cross-questioned any facts presented by the guides, strongly implying that visitors are seldom conscious of, or worried about, the manipulation of the past that interpretation implies: they consume the facts without questioning their validity.

The guides on the tour buses are trained so that they are qualified to narrate the city with a degree of historical accuracy. A guide said that they do try to avoid making direct political statements, but this should not mean that 'we shy away from giving information on the Parliament, devolution or British monarchy, we are free to inform anything as long as they (tourists) enjoy their tour', says a guide. They do not have to read a set script and are free to interpret their way, according to one guide. The bus goes through defined routes that limit the guides' control over the selection of sites, but they do use their discretion on what to emphasise during their tour. Apart from standard information, they also present contradictory and controversial issues. For example, a guide said to me,

> The story of Edinburgh is full of contradictions. It is a contrast between old town and new town, poverty and wealth, beauties and disasters, dignity and disgrace like parliament, trams and so on.

Additionally, guides also realise that their narratives keep many monuments alive, as they often suggest visitors take pictures of or take tours around monuments. Scholars have noted that tourist activities have increased the impulse towards heritage preservation. This helps in two ways. First, it helps in the revival of forgotten stories by giving economic viability to these heritage attractions, and second, it offers visitors a contemporary explanation of the past (Lowenthal, 2005).

Importantly, heritage preservation has an ideological role, as societies, cultural groups and governments collectively interpret the past in a subjective manner to meet their own ideological goals (Timothy & Boyd, 2003). The preservation and presentation of heritage and historic buildings and monuments therefore signifies what is apparent beneath the surface. There is a deeper interest than just the aesthetic ornamentation of a nation's pride or expression of identity or existence alone. It is the underlying message for which historic monuments signify more than just physical attractions, in which particular ideologies are conserved and represented for tourists. These messages can be transmitted by guides through interpretation while touring museums, historic houses, monuments and markers, tours, heritage districts, tourism landscapes and other public spaces (Hall, 2003). The point here is that it is through these artefacts and monuments that an image of a nation is created because guides assemble various resources of the nation that help frame its image and represent its story, which is a powerful way in which the 'national' existence is reasserted. Smith (1995) recognises that a nation has no existence outside its imagery and representations; and a guide, as a middleman, brokers this representation through the assembly of a 'national' iconography and interpretation. The role of the guide is analogous to that of 'nationalists' who similarly assemble artefacts, heritage and other resources to reconstruct their version of the 'national' story.

Conclusions

We have seen in this chapter that guides create a distinctive image of Scotland with vivid narratives. These narratives are full of resources that assert the existence of Scotland as a nation. The guides' account revolves around the stories of the Scottish Parliament, Edinburgh Castle, Scotland's ancient nationhood and military heritage. These are the potent symbols of Scottish nationhood and an inseparable part of its national identity.

The narratives produced by the guides in these tour buses offer visible impressions of the country to visitors. What is also important is that guides do not only present the facts associated with the sites or related stories but what they also present is an expressive discourse about their own feelings and attitudes towards the site (Jacobson, 1960). The guides' assertion of the key tenets of Scottish identity can be said to be directed towards producing a particular gaze and narrative that enhances the historical reality of the Scottish nation because 'we grasp the meanings of the nation through the images it casts, the symbols it uses and the fictions it evokes, in the novels, plays, poems, operas, ballads, pamphlets and newspapers which a literate reading public eagerly devours' (Smith, 1995: 7). Tour guiding can also be added to this list because it is open to anyone and what guides relate is important in producing the nation because, according to Bhabha (1990), nations are, after all, narratives.

Alderson and Low (1985) claim that good interpretation allows the visitor to understand the history and significance of events, people and objects with which a site is associated. Scotland's unique status of being a nation vying for its own state gives guides room for using interpretation as a tool for bolstering its status, which constant references to parliament and issues of devolution show. This also strengthens the idea that tourist sites are an appropriate place for locating the broader debate over self and society. According to Edensor (1997a, 1997b), the sites direct us to where people are at work making meaning, situating themselves in relation to public spectacle and making a biography that provides some coherency between self and world. The examples of the English vis-à-vis Scots distinction help us understand how Scottish society identifies itself with the closest 'other'.

What can be seen from the narratives produced on the tour buses is that the landmarks, monuments and stories in the heritage sites and other places on the bus tour routes are importunately flagging Scottish nationhood, which gets its narratives from the guides' accounts. According to Billig's (1995) idea of nationalism, nation is indicated, or 'flagged', in the lives of its citizenry every day. In fact Smith (1995: 7) notes that for post-modernists, 'the nation has become a cultural artefact of modernity, a system of collective imaginings and symbolic representations'. The guides in this case are not only representing the nation through interpretations, but as 'mediators' of both past and present they are presenting a particular communal past. Most notably, like archaeologists, they are excavating the remains of the past, and reconstructing them to relate to the present. Like nationalists, what they recount on the tour is that the Scottish nation was always there and they remind the visitor of their glorious past. The examples in this chapter closely correlate to that shown by Zuelow (2005) in the case of Irish tourism. He argues that tourism helped shape the presentation of Irish culture, history and landscape in post-civil war Ireland, thereby creating effectively a distinctive Irish identity. In order to do this Ireland selectively mobilised its heritage to emphasise its difference from England and the Empire, 'as part of its attempt to decolonise' (McManus, 2005: 237).

Aitchison (1999) believes that nationalism and militarism help to provide the connections between the past and the present or between the familiar and 'the other'. Militarism forms a significant part of the Edinburgh bus tours. In the case of Scotland, militarism on the tour functions as an important way of showing Scotland as something that is different, and that this differentness is entwined with Scottish nationalism. Militarism in Scotland often dates back to the pre-Union era. It tries to capture the Scottish past, which is distant, and give it continuity. Edensor (1997a) believes the shift towards the manufacture of an 'experience' in the presentation of the past produces a form of remembrance that depends less on legislative authority and more on an authenticity of feeling, of sensual experience. What we have seen in this chapter is that guides are not coerced by legislative duty but driven by their own judgement and feelings. For Billig (1995) the imagining of a 'country' involves the imagining of a bounded totality beyond immediate experience of place. The narrative helps frame this imagination beyond the tour buses because, in their touristic behaviour, 'tourists are the agents of semiotics, all over the world they are engaged in reading cities, landscapes and cultures as sign systems (Culler, 1988: 155). The account offered by the guides on the tour buses shows us that this reading of tourists is framed within a discourse which places Scottish nationhood in the centre.

A common thread that links all the four tenets of Scottish national identity discussed in this chapter is history. It is through the references to history that most of the guides recount the ancient Scottish nation. The resources of history are important in conferring an identity to a nation. But the use of history cannot be free from a larger 'national' context. We will see in the next chapter how history is selectively mobilised by some actors and how the promoters of heritage are recreating a version that is bestowing a uniform identity on a region despite the fact that the region has its distinctive historical experiences. I will look into this using a historical figure and an iconic king – Robert the Bruce – who is highly revered and linked to Scottish nationalism, and the example of an event: selling Highland culture as the region's distinctiveness.

5 Robert the Bruce and the Regional Heritage of the South-West

Introduction

I will now examine how heritage icons represent regional tourism and the role they play in the manifestation of regional identity. I will examine this through the study of some of the recently developed heritage tourism products in the south-west region. These products are encouraging the promotion of the dominant heritage of Scotland, largely marginalising the existing heritage of the region. This chapter looks into the cases of the heritage of Robert the Bruce, which stresses Scotland's militaristic tradition, the organisation of the Border Gathering event, which showcases Highland culture, and the marginalisation of the Covenanting heritage of the south-west of Scotland. I will argue that the promotion of a dominant heritage is meaningfully directed towards forming a uniform and homogenous identity, and that the introduction of this dominant heritage in the region is important because it encourages commonality within Scotland, which plays a part in reflecting Scottish nationalism.

There are three themes that run throughout this chapter. First is the role of history in the construction of cultural community. History has been an important resource in Scottish tourism. Durie *et al.* (2006) believe that history serves as a source for creating a sense of place for tourists in Scotland because it represents authenticity, and touring becomes a narration of a journey which is founded on the stories, places and people of Scotland. This chapter shows that the dominant heritage of Scotland has disinherited the distinctive historical experiences of a region. The selection of heritage by various agencies in Scottish tourism is not always rooted in local history; the narration produced by tourism is divorced from local historical reality and has most often failed to acknowledge the multiplicity of 'internal dissonant and dissident histories' (Dochery, 2004: 232): too little emphasis is given to the competing claims within Scotland regarding Scottish national identity (Finlay, 1999).

The second is the role of cultural events in the articulation and strengthening of community identity (Smith & Forest, 2006). Festivals and cultural events have been recognised as a source of group identity and place identity (de Bres & Davis, 2001). This is true in events which are staged to showcase aspects of a culture's heritage or re-enact a specific historically significant episode in a locality's history. The representation of cultural heritage in events and festivals creates a unique set of interactions between landscapes, local communities, tourists and heritage organisations (De Bres & Davis, 2001) and as such they celebrate and reaffirm some aspect of a culture's local, regional or national history and sense of place in the world (Carnegie & McCabe, 2008: 352). However, representations are often selective and not always appropriate. This is why many scholars have acknowledged that events can help local culture to be recreated as national culture (Crespi-Vallbona & Richards, 2007: 115). However, contrary to the above, this chapter discusses an event in which generic national culture is localised through the cultural event.

The third theme we will discuss later in this chapter is the form of tourism that is associated with visiting places of atrocity and remembrance, which has witnessed increased interest from scholars and is assigned different terms, such as dark tourism (Foley & Lennon, 1996); thanatourism (Seaton, 1996), or morbid tourism (Blom, 2000). Seaton (1996) classifies such tourism activity into five categories: to witness public enactments of death; to sites of individual or mass deaths; to memorials or internment sites; to see symbolic representation of death; and to witness re-enactments of death. Though scholars agree that this form of travel is relatively recent, people have long been drawn, purposefully or otherwise, towards sites, attractions or events linked in one way or another with death, suffering, violence or disaster (Stone, 2005). This is true in the case of Scotland, which has many heritage tourism sites associated with death or violence, like Bannockburn or Culloden, or even Edinburgh Castle, which was once used to house prisoners. Even the south-west region is not completely alien to the concept. In one of the earliest references to dark tourism concepts, Rojek (1993) mentions people flocking to Lockerbie, the crash site of Pan Am 103, in 1988 as an example of such activity. However, there is no such tourism in Lockerbie at present. Despite a strong association with this type of heritage in Scotland dominating tourism attractions, we note in this chapter that the heritage of the south-west region, which also has a strong association with this kind of heritage, is not properly identified as such and largely remains neglected.

Schouten (1995) believes that heritage is a contemporary interpretation of history which is subject to fashion, taste, ideology and personal preferences. Most importantly, it often has a tenuous connection to actual events, to history and the past: that is to say, our interpretation is formed in the context of the present (McCrone *et al.*, 1995). This chapter shows how tourism is introducing a more identifiable heritage, though relatively alien to the region's history which does not conform to the popular and dominant image of Scotland. Tourism is introducing a new identity to the region by rediscovering and recreating heritages. The two recent endeavours that I will focus upon in this chapter have tried to place the region's heritage on the tourism map through a more accepted legacy of Robert the Bruce and the Border Gathering. Robert the Bruce was the king of Scotland who successfully defeated the English at the battle of Bannockburn and secured Scotland its independence from England in 1320. He is a Scottish national hero and an important icon of Scottish national identity. The Border Gathering is an annual tourism event aimed at showcasing Scottish heritage to tourists. It is organised in a small town in the south-west of Scotland. I will also take note of the case of the regional heritage of Covenanting, which remains neglected and has failed to arouse any stimuli to tourism in the region. The heritage of Robert the Bruce and Highland traditions are proven icons that conform to the image of Scotland as a nation and are gaining more prominence on the region's tourism map as a result of promotional efforts.

A Brief Biography of Robert the Bruce

Robert the Bruce was born on 11 July 1274 at Turnberry Castle, Ayrshire (Scotland) as the son of Robert de Bruce, sixth Lord of Annandale; though it is widely believed in Dumfries and Galloway that he was born in Lochmaben in this region. He was distantly related to the Scottish royal family through his father. Bruce's grandfather was one of the claimants to the Scottish throne during a succession dispute in 1290–1292, which arose after the death of Alexander III of Scotland in 1286. Alexander III left as his heir a three-year-old granddaughter, Margaret, Maid of Norway. In accordance with the customs of the realm, the temporary control of the Kingdom of Scotland went to the Guardians of Scotland, who had been appointed to govern during the interregnum. An arrangement was made for Margaret to marry Edward of Caernarfon, Prince of Wales, infant heir to England and that he would later succeed as Edward II of both kingdoms.

Steps were also taken to protect the liberties of Scotland in the event of the union of the crowns by the signing of the Treaty of Birghum-Northampton in 1290. Amongst other points, the treaty contained the provision that although any offspring of this marriage would be heir to the crowns of both England and Scotland, the latter kingdom should be 'separate, apart and free in itself without subjection to the English Kingdom' (Scott, 1999: 21). It was categorically agreed that the laws, liberties and customs of Scotland were to be observed at all times; the great offices of state were to be held only by Scotsmen; no church matters were to be subject to interference from outside the kingdom; no parliament dealing with Scottish affairs was to be held outside the kingdom. All of these provisions were clearly intended to keep Scotland as an independent entity.

But the death of Margaret in 1290, before the marriage, gave rise to a danger of civil war in Scotland between two leading Scottish aristocratic factions, the Bruces and the Comyns. The English King, Edward I, was asked to arbitrate and John Balliol was chosen to be king. Both Bruce and his father refused to back Balliol and supported Edward I's invasion of Scotland in 1296 to force Balliol to abdicate. Edward then ruled Scotland as a province of England.

However, a resistance started against Edward amongst the lower ranks of the gentry, notably Andrew Moray and William Wallace. Bruce then supported William Wallace's uprising against the English. After Wallace was defeated at Falkirk in 1298, Bruce's lands were not confiscated, and in 1298, Bruce became a guardian of Scotland, with John Comyn, Balliol's nephew and Bruce's greatest rival for the Scottish throne. Early in 1306, Bruce and Comyn agreed to meet in Greyfriars Church at Dumfries for an agenda that is not clearly known. But there arose an argument that reached a sudden and violent climax when Bruce fatally stabbed Comyn. The news of the murder reached Edward after a few days, and Bruce made an appeal of some sort to Edward, threatening to defend himself 'with the longest stick that he had' if his appeal was unsuccessful (McNamee, 1997: 29). Duncan thinks that Bruce demanded a comprehensive pardon to shield him from the fury of the Comyns (Duncan, 1992). Despite his appeal, Bruce was outlawed. After securing a couple of castles in the south-west, Bruce proclaimed his right to the throne, and on 27 March was crowned king at Scone. However, the following year Edward's army deposed him and forced him to flee. His wife and daughters were imprisoned and three of his brothers executed. It is believed he spent the winter on an island off the coast of Antrim (Northern Ireland).

Returning to Scotland, Robert waged a guerrilla war against the new King Edward II, son of Edward I of England. His war against the English reached its climax on 23 June 1314 at the Battle of Bannockburn, where

Edward II led a force of over 20,000 men to end the Scots' siege of Stirling Castle. Bruce was waiting for them with 9000 men. Bruce secured his historic defeat over the English army at the battle, confirming the re-establishment of an independent Scottish monarchy. Even after Bannockburn and the Scottish capture of Berwick in 1318, Edward II refused to give up his claim to the overlordship of Scotland. In 1320, the Scottish earls, barons and the 'community of the realm' sent a letter known as the 'Declaration of Arbroath' to Pope John XXII declaring that Robert the Bruce was their rightful monarch and requesting him to confirm Scotland's status as an independent, sovereign state, with a right to defend itself against attack. Four years later, Bruce was finally recognised as king of an independent Scotland.

The Franco-Scottish alliance was renewed in the Treaty of Corbeil in 1326, which confirmed the obligation of each state to join the other in declaring war if either was attacked by England. In 1327, Edward II was deposed in favour of his son and peace was made with Scotland. This included a total renunciation of all English claims to superiority over Scotland. On 7 June 1329, Robert the Bruce died and was buried at Dunfermline.

The story of Bruce is important in the understanding of Scottish nationhood. The historian Barrow (1988) argues that the 13th century saw the first emergence of 'Scotland' in a modern sense. The 'community of realm' was 'conscious of political ideas and capable of constructive political action in years of difficulty and danger' (Duncan, 1966: 184). According to Barrow (1988) Scotland devolved a political identity and nationhood during the peaceful 13th century. The importance of Bruce is that he, as the king, identified himself with that nationhood and accomplished a political revolution.

Robert the Bruce as Heritage Attraction

It can be said that Dumfries and Galloway is integral to Robert the Bruce's struggle to gain the Scottish throne as he hailed from the south-west region. The area was of strategic importance to Scotland as it held the western of the two principal routes into the country from England. Nithsdale and Annandale, and, to some extent, Esksdale, offered natural routes into the heart of Scotland. Armies from both sides criss-crossed the area throughout the years of resistance. There are many places in the region that are historically associated with Bruce. For example, Clatteringshaws, where there is a stone commemorating the Battle of Raploch in 1307. A huge boulder is marked as the 'Bruce Stone', which identifies it as a site where the king rested after the battle. Dumfries has many places associated with Bruce, such as

Dumfries Castle which stood in what is now Castledykes Park, and the famous Church of the Greyfriars, which has long since disappeared but where there is a plaque commemorating the Comyn murder.

Robert the Bruce is a national hero and a strong icon of Scottish identity. He is effectively used in tourism by other regions, for example Sterling and Bannockburn. Indeed, his image is so strongly bound up with his success in the battle of Bannockburn near Stirling that the place identity of Stirling has been largely created by historical memories associated with him. However, some commentators argue that the place identity of Stirling is manufactured by tourism with the help of a nationalist discourse (Aitchison, 1999). Much of this has happened because of the legacy of Robert the Bruce and others, showcased to tourists as an attraction in and around Stirling, the central attraction of which is the Bannockburn battle site that also houses a heritage centre dedicated to Bruce (Figure 5.1). Together with Bannockburn, the presence of the Wallace Monument and Stirling Castle make Stirling, as Lannon (1983: 56) describes it, the 'seed-box' of Scottish nationalism (cited in Edensor, 1997a).

In 1999 the Robert the Bruce Commemoration Trust was founded in Dumfries with the aim of furthering the heritage of Robert the Bruce in the south-west region. The main aim of the trust is to establish a living history visitor centre in Dumfriesshire dedicated to Scotland's hero king. The trust declares its purpose is to celebrate the history and heritage of the king, to provide educational and tourism opportunities and a much needed indoor

Figure 5.1 Robert the Bruce statue at Bannockburn

attraction for the public and tourists. This is important because, as some of the responses of the trustees show, they have a strong sense of Scottish nationalism that resonates with the political implication this has for the Union, suggesting that the development of Robert the Bruce heritage is not only related to tourism alone: it is also simultaneously showcasing Scotland's potent political icon and has an underlying political motive.

As a precursor to their longer-term goal, the trust has developed and launched the Robert the Bruce Trail throughout Dumfries and Galloway in 2009, with a project cost of over £60,000. There are four trails and three of them – The Eastern Trail, The Central Trail and The Western Trail – are driving trails, which are over 100-miles long and require at least three hours of driving time each. The fourth, the Dumfries Town Trail, is a walking trail spanning approximately three miles and taking about three hours. These trails link 30 sites closely associated with Bruce and the Wars of Independence. All sites are marked by explanatory plaques. The trust has also compiled booklets and leaflets explaining the sites which are distributed across the region through various outlets, such as local libraries, tourist information centers, museums and other visitor attractions. According to one of its members, providing educational history and enhancing tourists' local experience are two important reasons for developing the trail. This is not unique given the fact that a successful heritage tourism product is an interpretation of local historical experience insofar as it can be related to, and incorporated in, the historical experience of the visitor (Ashworth, 1994). The chairman of the trust confirms that the trails fulfill this dual purpose. They can enhance the tourist experience of Dumfries and Galloway and, at the same time, give people the opportunity to learn more about the man who, in the chairman's view, was arguably the greatest ever Scotsman. He says with pride, 'King Robert the Bruce was the man who forged Scotland into the nation we are today'. The trail brochure brings a reference to history into the trail. It states, 'Journey back 700 years to the Wars of Independence and see Dumfries and Galloway through the eyes of Scotland's greatest King.'

When the author made an observational visit to some of the heritage sites on the trail, they looked more or less abandoned and deserted. There were no visitors in any of the Bruce-related areas in the town of Lochmaben and its surroundings. The chairman of the trust was confident that the trails would start getting visitors gradually over the next few tourist seasons. In 2009 it was said that the heritage trails were in the initial period of being launched, so visitor numbers could only be expected to reach significant levels from the summer of 2010, when the visitor season restarted in the region. However, repeat visits were made in summer 2011 and again in 2013 and there was no remarkable tourism activity observed.

Edensor states that Bruce is a historical as well as a mythical figure and has argued that his heroic mythical status has lately been used for political purposes at Bannockburn. Whether Robert the Bruce is a mythical figure or not is a debatable issue but there is an agreement that the political potency of Bannockburn makes it an important icon of Scottish nationalism (McCrone *et al.*, 1995). The mythical nature of a heritage icon gives room for manipulation in the construction and representation of identity. This means that identity is not engrained in history per se but is more a reference to history or the popular ideas about history that achieve mythical status (Smout, 1994). Smout (1994) says that, more than actual history, it is the mythical stories that tell the history that are important in the construction of national identity: for example, the story that the Scots defeated the English at the battle of Bannockburn and ensured Scottish independence; that the Highland Clearances were a tragic episode carried out by Anglicised lairds; that the battle of Culloden was followed by English atrocities against the Scots, all have an important bearing on the creation of Scottish identity.

According to Selwyn (1996), myth assumes a greater role in the debate about what constitutes a nation because of the absence of any 'real entity' as nation; and makes the nation itself a myth. The absence of substantive reliable historical documents of his period makes Bruce also a mythical rather than a historical figure alone. Despite contested details of his origin, the trust is trying to create a favourable version of history to claim him for the region. The Robert the Bruce Commemoration Trust claims,

> Bruce's connections with the southwest of Scotland stretched right across the region... although there is a *claim* that he was born at Lochmaben, most historians think it more *likely* that Turnberry Castle would have been the place of his birth... It is *likely* he spent much of his time on the run in the mountains and forests of Dumfries and Galloway and Ayrshire. After all they were his lands by 1306 and he could count on his friends and subjects for help and information. (Emphasis added)

This shows us the trust's uncertainty of the historical facts. It relies on tales to justify itself in the selection of Dumfries as a location for a visitor centre. It asks, 'Why Dumfries?' The answer according to the trust is, 'simply because Bruce's quest for the throne of Scotland started in the town with the slaying of his cousin, John "The Red" Comyn, Lord of Badenoch' (The Bruce Trust, 2009).

Upon speaking with some of the members of the trust it became apparent that the establishment of the visitor centre dedicated to Bruce is not outside the ambit of the nation's political ambition. The use of the icon of Scottish national stature serves a dual purpose: first it helps bring the south-west region closer to the Scottish national mainstream and, second, it serves a political purpose. A trustee says,

> it is essential to link all the regions of the vast area with one historic character. The region is often 'forgotten' by central government because of its distance from Edinburgh but Bruce's War of Independence resonates proudly with the aims of the current Scottish Parliament and should keep Dumfries and Galloway in their minds.

This remark is important for us to understand the political importance of Bruce's heritage to the south-west. By associating the region with Robert the Bruce, the trustee believes the region can achieve an identity which is more acceptable and can appeal more convincingly to parliament, which is led by Nationalists, helping the south-west region to gain attention from the centre, that is, Edinburgh. For the trustee it is imperative that bringing Bruce closer to the region helps the region move closer to the centre. Another trustee makes a further attempt to bring Bruce to the region by claiming, 'He grew up here. The nation of Scotland was forged here.'

We have observed in Chapter 2 that Scotland never dissolved its identity with England even after becoming part of the Union. Many scholars have accepted that Scottish identity is often manifested in opposition to, or in relation to, England. A comment from another trustee confirms this. He feels that 'Scots like to think of themselves as different from the English both in historic and cultural ideals and a role model such as Bruce fits this perfectly.'

The imagination of Scottish nationhood is dominated by Bruce's reference and his statue at Bannockburn assumes centre-stage. There is also a statue erected to Robert the Bruce in the town centre of Lochmaben in the south-west, where one story suggests he was born (Figure 5.2). This was erected in 1879. But it is the statue of him at Bannockburn that dominates the media representation of Bruce, despite the fact that it was unveiled only relatively recently, in June 1964, to mark the 650th anniversary of the battle of Bannockburn. A trustee recognises the importance of Bruce in the media. He believes that promoting Bruce's heritage in the region should help to boost the media representation of the region. He adds, 'There is a limit to what TV can do by way of documentation, but tourism can be promoted in several media forms.' The other members are also aware that tourism can appear in several media forms as it uses various print and electronic communication mediums in promoting a destination. The mediatised role tourism plays in promoting an icon is manifested in the trust's main objective that lays down establishing the 'state of the art' visitor centre as its ultimate goal.

Figure 5.2 Robert the Bruce statue at Lochmaben town centre

A prevalent mode of tourist gazing is the 'mediatised gaze', shaped by re-branded places and re-presentations of heritage which draw upon film and television programmes (Urry, 2002: 151). Edensor (2005) has shown through the case of William Wallace how mediated forms mix into a dense matrix or resource bank which reinforces his iconic significance but permits a wide range of appropriation and experience. The Bruce Trail brochure developed by the trust tries to capture the popular image of Bruce, using his mediated image by mentioning the Hollywood blockbuster *Braveheart*. The brochure starts,

> If you have watched 'Braveheart', you will know it is based on the story of William Wallace's fight for Scotland's freedom from English oppression in medieval times. The film ends with Wallace's execution in 1305, but the epilogue shows the subsequent victory by King Robert the Bruce at Bannockburn. The Robert the Bruce Trail tells the story of how a nobleman from south west Scotland gained the nation's crown and recovered her freedom.

Robert the Bruce's success at the battle of Bannockburn makes him the central figure in the iconography of Scottish national heroes. This also links him inextricably to Scottish nationhood, because the victory at Bannockburn asserted Scottish nationhood. This is recognised by a number of trustees: 'He was able to forge a Scottish identity for the first time. Without the effort of Bruce, Scotland would only have been a region of England.' Another trustee states, 'Scotland's history as a nation and its survival is strongly tied to Bruce.' Another trustee believes Bruce's heritage is very important to the region: 'with hindsight to a "semi-separate only" identity he secured us independent status'.

By attaching strong emphasis to Bruce's success in gaining Scotland its independence, the trustees are testifying that they are driven not only by the touristic potential of his heritage but also a political potential of his legacy. For the members of the trust, tourism is the means to spread his legacy. These ideas of the trustees however are not new. The Bannockburn heritage centre at Stirling shows a documentary of the battle of Bannockburn to instil a sense of pride (Edensor, 1997b; McCrone *et al.*, 1995). An information officer at the Bannockburn heritage centre describes the documentary:

> It is about the Battle of Bannockburn. Basically 1314 was the time when Bannockburn came ... from that day Scotland is free ... that is why Scottish people have more words in the Parliament; that's why they can decide things. If they had not won this battle of Bannockburn it seemed that we should call it not Scotland but England. Bannockburn is what stands for Scotland's freedom ... that's why this can be a separate country. (Personal communication, April 2008)

The Border Gathering

The Border Gathering started as a small event in 1996. It has now evolved as an annual tourist event that celebrates Scottish heritage in the region. The person who pioneered the event states the motive behind its conception, 'The Border Gathering was conceived to celebrate the heritage and culture of borderland. This region is different than other places: there are many things to do, to promote and enjoy heritage which was not promoted enough.' The Border Gathering event website states, it 'is an annual event hosted in the beautiful countryside of South West Scotland, consisting of a celebration of Border culture' (The Border Gathering, 2009).

The gathering is a cultural event, designed for overseas visitors, to showcase local heritage. The event website makes the case for the event by recognising this:

> But it is the cultural heritage that makes this country very special. For four days, the Border Gathering will show you this culture – the music in many forms – the dance, both present and past – the Games, a trial of strength for the chief to choose his strongest men for defence. You will

learn some of the fascinating history, and visit the beautiful country side and castles and mansions of bonnie Galloway. This is the land of the Border Reiver, the home of many clans and families.

Though named as an event of borderland heritage, it can best be described as a synthesis of the Highland tradition in Lowland territory. The use of words such as 'Gathering', 'Games', 'Clan' in the promotional media of the event implies Highland sporting events, epitomising Scottish Highland culture. The general format of the event over the last few years has been stretched over four days. The first three days cover a historical symposium, music concerts, sightseeing and other historical talks. The final and main event is the 'Border Games and Country Festival', which is designed as a typical Highland games event and is organised in a large open playing field. There are mainly Highland sporting events. Visitors are often seen in their clan tartans and the majority of the other events that take place are more akin to Highland games. The gathering features 'Highland Games, Highland Dancing and Piping Competitions', as major attractions amongst other events happening simultaneously (The Border Gathering, 2009). Most of the games and events are related to traditional war skills and battle re-enactment (Figure 5.3). This is meaningful because re-enactment events aim to recreate objects and seek to interpret them in ways that attribute social purpose, cultural attitudes and moralities to the individual and groups involved (Carnegie & McCabe, 2008).

Some stalls with local and regional produce are also displayed. However, the main feature of the gathering is not regional, but the Highland Games 'Heavies', in which athletes participate in categories like 'putting the shot',

Figure 5.3 War re-enactment at Border Gathering event

Figure 5.4 Highland games at Border Gathering event

'putting the heavy stane', 'weight distance' and 'hammer throw' (Figure 5.4). It also includes piping competitions and Highland dancing competitions. The Border Gathering each year features a particular clan from the region. 'This year we honour the name of Johnstone, one of the major clans of the Borderland', states the event brochure for 2008 (The Border Gathering, 2008). Clan or clanship, which gives priority to militaristic values of courage, loyalty, obedience and communal cohesion rather than personal acquisitiveness, competition and individualism, is strongly associated with the Highlands (Devine, 1999).

As a border event it is promoted more in line with Highland cultural events, which are popular in places where large numbers of Scottish émigrés are residing and are aimed at them. The primary market of the Border Gathering event is the Scottish diaspora from the United States and Canada (personal communication with the promoter). The distinctiveness of the Highlands as an atypical cultural entity is derived from unique features of its culture, such as clanship, tartan, pipers and so on. As Hugh Trevor-Roper (1983: 15) states,

> Today, whenever Scotchmen gather together to celebrate their national identity, they assert it openly by certain distinctive national apparatus. They wear the kilt, woven in tartan whose colour and pattern indicates their 'clan'; and if they indulge in music, their instrument is the bagpipe.

It can be argued the event is organised to celebrate the popular version of Scottish national identity rather than to promote regional culture and traditions. The promoter of the event acknowledges the nationalistic character of the event but dissociates it from any political inclinations. '(I)t is difficult. It is different. You do not become political by being a nationalist. Being nationalist can be and should be free from politics. It is indeed difficult to separate politics here. You do not have to be political to be a nationalist.' The disassociation with politics is not unusual if we consider that idea that festivals are contested fields of meaning because different groups of 'stakeholders' try to utilise the symbolic capital of the event for their own ends (Crespi-Vallbona & Richards, 2007: 103).

The attempt to use Highland tradition to promote regional events is important in three senses. First, the continuous success of the event over these years proves the point that the popular image of Scotland is that of the Highlands. Second, the selling of this image in the south-west region, which has its own distinctive culture, is a typical example of cultural commodification. The Highland culture here is imported and resold as local. Third, the increasing popularity and scale of an event of this type is influential in building a new heritage that has a tendency to confer a newer identity to the region. Since the most potent form of Scottish national identity resides in the Highland tradition, bestowing this identity on the region is directed towards homogenisation of national culture and uniform identity.

The Covenanting Heritage of the South-West Region

The term 'Covenanters' refers to people who refused to accept a Royal decree that King Charles I was head of the church. Those people signed a covenant in 1637 which stated that only Jesus Christ could command such a position. The government retaliated by capturing and punishing, and often executing, those who refused to adhere to the king's religious superiority. The Scottish Covenanting movement as a national movement of opposition lasted from 1639 until 1688. The period of extreme persecution is often referred to as 'The Killing Times'. Monuments were later laid in commemoration of those who were killed during the movement.

Many scholars believe that covenants and the Covenanters have always been at the forefront of Scottish historiography, but they complain that there is a very limited amount of reputed scholarship devoted to this theme in Scotland (Cowan, 1968). Covenanting was a great national movement in Scotland (Stevenson, 1988). According to Stevenson, the support was not universal, but the participation of most of those forming the dominant elites in society – nobles and other landowners, burgesses and parish ministers – and the widespread support at the popular level provide ample justification for defining the movement as a 'national' one. He also believes that the movement was 'national' because central to it was the preservation of Scotland's national identity, and the Reformation of 1560 was a key to this because at the heart of the Reformation was the rejection of the international authority of the Pope in religion, the claiming of the rights of the nation to control the church without outside interference (Stevenson, 1988; also see Burrell, 1964).

The south-west was the heartland of Covenanting (Lynch, 2005; Hearn, 2000). According to the Scottish Covenanting Memorial Association, there are around 50 Covenanting memorials in Dumfries and Galloway. Additionally there are 50 recognised memorials in the adjoining region of Ayrshire (personal communication). Despite the claim that most of Scotland's tourism resources are the product of history, there is no significant tourism activity around this resource, which is part of a potent local history. Interestingly, tourism activities that are designed to explore the unique and local heritage of Covenanting, which is believed to be indigenous and 'arising out of Scottish society' (Cowan, 2002: 122), are almost non-existent. The regional website of VisitScotland does not have any mention of Covenanting heritage in its promotional pages. There has been a tiny effort by local heritage groups who have tried to produce a brief information booklet of Covenanting memorials in their locality; it is not of a professional standard and has no commercial interest. The only remarkable organisation looking into Covenanting heritage is the 'Scottish Covenanter Memorials Association' established in 1966, which within its limited resources has been doing its best to protect, restore or replace monuments and memorials to the Covenanters. However, it is not driven by a tourism objective. As a result there is hardly any effective tourism activity to capture this significant heritage. The only serious endeavour has been to promote a Covenanting Trail by producing a promotional brochure for the Nithsdale Covenanting Trail in 1986, marking the octocentenary of the town of Dumfries, but this has not received any attention since that time and the brochure can now only be found in a drawer of a local archive.

Covenanting was a religious event, but its contemporary significance for tourism is that '(C)ovenanting monuments represent Scotland's first war memorials' (Cowan, 2002: 136). It is also important to note that as a tourism product there is plenty of interest in the Covenanting phenomenon. Some of the visitors of Scottish descent whom this researcher interviewed were informed about and interested in visiting the Covenanting memorials as a part of their tour (see Chapter 7). Even if it was to assume that Covenanting represented a darker side of Scottish history, Miles (2012), who has examined the deeper meanings thought to be attached to places of suffering and death, suggests that the commercialisation of 'darker' sites results in a lessening of the visceral type of experience. In terms of tourism, there is ever-increasing curiosity in this type of travel (Lennon & Foley, 2000). For example, Sharpley and Stone (2009) mention that the dark tourism academic website www.dark-tourism.org.uk annually receives over 60,000 hits.

The absence of Covenanting heritage in the region's tourism can be contrasted with other stronger historical images, though not produced locally, such as castles and abbeys, which form the dominant image of Scotland. Not mentioning regional heritage, the regional tourist board website tries to present the dominant version of Scotland when it says, 'Dumfries & Galloway is a region steeped in history. From stone circles and chambered cairns over four millennia old, the arrival of Christianity in Scotland, to medieval castles and battles for Scottish independence' (VisitScotland Dumfries and Galloway, 2009). For some people, a reason for not promoting Covenanter history, apart from the fact that it is grim, is that those working in tourism are not interested in religious matters and think it would be a 'turn-off'; specifically, if we consider the south-west region's proximity to Northern Ireland and its bitter Catholic–Protestant conflict might make the subject uncomfortable. However, also, it cannot be denied that the Covenanting heritage is inextricably linked to Scotland (Finlay, 1999), yet it does not form any part of contemporary Scotland's popular imagination, does not conform to Scotland's dominant image, is not embedded strongly within Scotland's national identity and thus could not stand on its own.

Conclusions

In this chapter I have shown how tourism is driven towards forging a new identity for the region of south-west Scotland by recreating heritage. The three cases of heritage tourism products in the region show that a dominant version of Scotland is transmitted through tourism. The production of the dominant version of Scottish history through Highland culture and militaristic tradition in the south-west region is the assertion of a historic past. The Scottish historic past produced in these narratives is a potent booster of Scottish nationalism. In the context of rising nationalism, the decline of local heritage, like that of Covenanting, may seem normal because rising populist nationalism tends to destroy traditional heritage (Lowenthal, 1998), but such an occurrence is meaningful since it can represent a move towards producing a uniform generic Scottish culture.

The development of Robert the Bruce as a tourist attraction in the region is an imported icon. It is a meaningful recreation of heritage, because despite his strong association with this region his heritage has remained largely neglected and not developed as a tourist attraction. Producing a uniform and generic Scottish identity by recreating newer heritages in the region stresses the particular character and uniqueness of Scotland. This uniqueness has come in the form of a dominant heritage, which in the case of the south-west of Scotland has also led to the marginalisation of local heritage. The production of a uniform, homogeneous culture is one of the ways through which nationhood becomes authenticated because these efforts portray the nation in a way that flatters and reinforces its national identity. The assertion of national identity is one of the important manifestations of nationalism in Scotland (Bechhofer & McCrone, 2009). Thus, this case study helps us to see that tourism as a cultural expression can be a tool to articulate nationalism.

There are pertinent reasons to argue that efforts to introduce national heritage to the region are an expression of nationalism. According to Rose (1995), all places are interpreted from particular social positions and for particular social reasons. The narrative of The Robert the Bruce Commemoration Trust and the Border Gathering is produced from a social position that places Scottish Highland imagery at the centre of Scottish national identity. Highland culture and tradition are well-worn expressions of Scottish nationalism but are not always the appropriate ones. Hall (1996) believes that identity invokes an origin in a historical past with which it continues to correspond and seeks to discover how it is being represented. Bringing history to the region has a dual purpose. It serves as a means to produce a narrative of the nation with the help of a stereotypical image of Scotland to visitors. Additionally, since representation is important in the articulation of a sense of place, showcasing Robert the Bruce and Highland heritage has the tendency to displace or further marginalise the events and episodes of the local history of the region. This process could also lead to the homogenisation of the historical and cultural narrative of the nation.

We must accept the fact that national identity need not be uniform and homogeneous: it can accommodate differences so long as it can postulate the 'existence of a collective subject – the nation' (Wright, 1985: 145). However, the argument in this chapter is that in the case of Scotland this homogenisation of heritage is rooted in the revived Scottish nationalism, which stresses commonalities rather than differences within Scotland (Smith, 1993). Since Highland culture figures as a major part of Scottish national identity (Withers, 1992), the promotion of this culture in the south-west, which has its own distinct history and traditions, is likely to steer towards the formation of a homogeneous heritage across the country.

According to MacGregor (1991), the point of heritage is not that the public should learn something, but that they should *become* something (cited in Lowenthal, 1998: 23). The predominant stress on Highland culture and images in the Border Gathering and the language of the trust encouraging visitors to journey back 700 years to see the region 'through Bruce's eyes' are examples of an attempt to turn the south-west into a more recognisable Scottish entity. This is to say that the heritage of Bruce and the display of Highland culture, tartan and kilt heritage in the south-west inspire visitors and people across the region to 'become Scots' and to view the region as typical of Scotland.

In the particular cases of Covenanting and Robert the Bruce heritage, it is acknowledged that both of them to some extent are rooted in the region. But the contrasting fate of Covenanting and Robert the Bruce heritage in tourism shows how the former is ignored and the latter is re-discovered in the region. The selection of what is to be ignored and what is to be rediscovered is driven by political potency as the views of some of the trustees indicate. This is also to conform to the political correctness of choosing Robert the Bruce in contemporary Scottish politics, since the Nationalists are in government and form the largest party in the current Scottish Parliament. It shows that the treatment of the two heritages is meaningful politically. Local heritage that is organic and communal does not fit into Scottish nationalism, is not driven towards commonalities and is marginalised; in contrast, heritage that coincides with nationalistic goals is endorsed. What can be construed from the above example is that the promotion of Highland culture and King Robert the Bruce as heritage in the south-west is an effort driven towards localising national heritage.

There are two important questions that emerge here. The first relates to the issue of the authenticity of the event; for instance, in the case of the Border Gathering, how authentic visitors think these events are. If visitors do not feel that the event is authentic it cannot have a deep bearing on the region's identity. But a study in North Carolina has shown that a vivid perception of authenticity can be achieved even when the event is staged in a place far away from the original source of the cultural tradition (Chhabra *et al.*, 2003). This chapter was limited in scope: I did not try to seek visitors' perceptions of the event and the conclusions were drawn from field observations and the representation of heritage, opinions expressed by the heritage promoters and other secondary sources. The second question concerns how one should look into the case of the Highland games that are held worldwide, which does not transform the host nation's national identity the way it does in Scotland. The holding of Highland games does not impose an identity, but it does give an opportunity for the people of Scottish descent to articulate their sense of self, which is a way to express their homeland nationalism. I will delve into this in Chapter 7 in greater detail.

In her historical account of Scotland's tourism, Grenier (2005) concludes that in the narrative of tourism, Scotland's history is presented as a loose collection of incidents with little sense of a unifying thread to emphasise Scottish distinctiveness, and downplays any threat posed by its independent past. The authority and appropriateness of Highland images have been criticised for their very failure to appreciate Scotland's diversity, and have been accused of 'dubious historical authenticity' (Grenier, 2005: 159). But as has been indicated earlier, Highland culture epitomises Scotland and the Highland games are also popular amongst visitors to Scotland. The Highland image forms the most potent version of Scotland's national identity (Withers, 1992). Because of its iconic value, it is strongly associated with the popular image of Scotland in tourism and is strongly embedded in the promotion of Scottish tourism (Butler, 1998). However, there can be non-political reasons for bringing Highland culture to the region. The intent of this chapter was to establish the cultural potency of the Highland identity in the overall identity of the Scottish nation. Like Robert the Bruce, another historical figure who commands equal importance in the iconography of Scottish national identity is Robert Burns. In the next chapter, we will see how the image and heritage of Robert Burns instil a sense of common national aspiration in the south-west region. We will see this through reading his legacy enshrined in the museums dedicated to him in the south-west region.

6 The Scottish Nation in the Cultural Heritage of Robert Burns

Introduction

The role of literary figures in enhancing Scottish nationhood and national identity is immense. There is a historical association between literature and Scotland. Cowan and Gifford (1999: 1) argue that literature and history in Scotland are 'polar twins', because they were indistinguishable at the beginning: the earliest historical sources were literary and the first Scottish poem was historical in content. Literary icons have drawn immense attention from travellers from the early period of Scottish tourism. We have already noted in the earlier chapters the role of Sir Walter Scott on various occasions. However, another literary figure who bears great significance in Scotland and beyond is Robert Burns, but his heritage in the articulation of Scottish nationhood has not been given due attention until now. The purpose of this chapter is to study the question of authenticity at the Robert Burns museum in the south-west region, and later to discuss how this authenticity conveys a connection with the sense of nationhood.

Robert Burns is Scotland's best-known poet; he was prolific, writing about 400 songs during his short life, though the extent of his authorship is still unknown. His literary genius and immense popularity have made him a strong marker of Scottish identity. Many organisations funded by the Scottish government market Burns extensively and, according to Macleod (2010: 81), 'he is an example of state-sanctioned national identity used as heritage attraction'. In this chapter I will examine Burns' cult status and look into the notion of authenticity in his heritage in the south-west region, arguing that his heritage in the region plays a semiotic role in presenting a symbolic version of Scottish national identity.

The semiotic role of tourism is recognised by MacCannell (1999), who calls tourism more than 'merely a collection of random material representations'. MacCannell (1999: 45) claims that, 'when they appear in itineraries, they have a moral claim on the tourists and, at the same time, they tend toward universality, incorporating natural, social, historical and cultural domains in a single representation made possible by the tour'. This instigates hosts – whether it be authorities or cultures that select objects for tourists' consumption – to present those aspects of their representations that they deem most appropriate and which they want to make more prominent. Pitchford (2006) has shown how museums and other attractions that focus on a group's history and culture serve as a medium to project ethnic and nationalist messages and help to build a revalued collective identity. This happens because, according to Culler (1988: 55), in their touristic behaviour, 'tourists are the agents of semiotics, all over the world they are engaged in reading cities, landscapes and cultures as sign systems'. Thus, tourism destinations do not only produce experiences, but through the consumption of the signs, they also produce a perception or a way of viewing the destination. Koshar (1998: 325) terms it an 'optics of tourism' that would allow visitors to make sense of the sights and events unfolding before them.

This is made clearer by MacCannell (1999), for whom, in the semiotic structure of tourism, reproductions like postcards, travel posters, miniature Eiffel Towers and the Statue of Liberty are markers. These markers represent sites to the tourist (MacCannell, 1999: 110). This would lead to converting anything of national, regional or local significance into an item on the itinerary of tourists, making tourism a replica of the nation's iconography. Touristic souvenirs take those national representations back home with the tourist. Reproduction in the form of touristic souvenirs means that the representation of a particular ideology is not confined within any spatial or temporal dimension. An act of tourism thus extends to more than that which the tourist encounters in his tour alone and travels beyond his destination (Rojek & Urry, 1997). MacCannell therefore calls tourism 'not just an aggregate of merely commercial activities', but also an 'ideological framing of history, nature, and tradition; a framing that has the power to reshape culture and nature to its own needs' (MacCannell, 1992). It is this 'ideological framing' that helps make tourism a commercially packaged expression of nationalism.

There are important reasons for associating Robert Burns museums with the idea of authenticity. Museums are important places where the semiotics of a nation can be presented. They are often seen as places to produce national discourse and can effectively be the venue for presenting a desired ideology: as an important component of heritage they are repositories of identity. Robert Burns-related museums are studied because, apart from being just a national poet, he is a national icon, standing to serve the interests of both tourism and national identity. In this way Burns sites are in effect semiotically symbolising national significance. Authenticity has not only remained a central theme in the study of tourism (Cohen, 1979; Cole, 2007; Crang, 1996; Hughes, 1995; MacCannell, 1999; Urry, 2006; Wang, 1999, 2000) but it also assumes greater significance in the contemporary debate on the future of Scottish tourism (Hall, 2007; King, 2007; Yeoman *et al.*, 2007). One reason, as King (2007) identifies, is because it is a tourism-dependent and identity-seeking nation and the other reason is the centrality of tourism in the understanding of Scotland.

In Scotland, museums bear a special relevance. McCrone (2002) notes that the founding of national museums was an important event in the capture of 'history', to showcase the nation's 'heritage' to its best advantage. However, McLean (2005) is of the opinion that the fluidity of national identity in an era of multiculturalism makes the task of museums challenging. This is because, unlike in the past, museums today, while narrating the nation, have the task of narrating its diversity. The study of the National Museum of Scotland makes it clear that museums are constructing multifarious readings that reflect both their individual identities and their collective identities (McLean & Cooke, 2003). They also find that in addition to the traditional 'mythic' identity of Scotland, museum visitors make contemporary readings of the museums' identities which are shaped by current political and cultural understandings of the nation of Scotland.

This chapter is based on observations at four museums in the south-west of Scotland which are dedicated to Burns-related places of interest. There are two main reasons for choosing them. First, because the poet spent the most significant part of his life in the south-west of Scotland where these museums are located, and second, because the literary associations are themselves a resource for authenticity, where some element of the original dwelling has been preserved and there are artefacts that can be dated to the author (Herbert, 2003). Three of these museums are exclusively dedicated to Burns and are based in houses formally occupied by the poet. The fourth is a recent construction and specially designed as a tourist attraction.

Robert Burns and His Heritage in the South-West of Scotland

Robert Burns was born on 25 January 1759 in Alloway, two miles south of Ayr, Scotland, as the first of the seven children of William Burnes and Agnes Broun. His parents were tenant farmers but they ensured their son received a relatively good education. He was taught initially by a private headmaster hired by his father and four neighbours at the village school. In the later years, the works of Alexander Pope, Henry Mackenzie and Laurence Sterne fired Burns' poetic impulse. Hard physical labour on the family farm took its toll on the young Burns, who increasingly turned his attentions towards the passions of poetry, nature, drink and women, which would characterise the rest of his life.

After a couple of earlier relationships, he fathered twins with his eventual wife Jean Armour, but a rift in their relationship nearly led to Burns emigrating as a plantation bookkeeper to Jamaica in 1786 with his lover 'Highland' Mary Campbell. To raise the funds for his passage to Jamaica he planned the publication of *Poems, Chiefly in the Scottish Dialect*. The Kilmarnock edition of this compendium received widespread praise. He postponed his Jamaican voyage as he planned for a second edition of his poems, but the death of Mary Campbell, possibly in premature childbirth, made the journey to Jamaica pointless to him and he considered other options, including a proposal to lease a farm near Dumfries. Henry Mackenzie reviewed his Kilmarnock edition in the *Lounger* in the same year and acclaimed Burns as 'this Heaven-taught ploughman' (Bold, 1991: 9).

After the success of the Kilmarnock edition he associated himself with James Johnson's *Scots Musical Museum*, for which he extensively travelled within Scotland. In March 1788 he signed a deal for Ellisland Farm and left Edinburgh for Mauchline, where he met a distressed Jean and married her; in September of the same year he started to work as an excise officer. But he was weary of working on the farm as well as his excise duties, which can be sensed in a letter written to his brother, 'This farm has undone my enjoyment of myself' (Bold, 1991: 9). In 1790 he was transferred to the Dumfries Third Division of Excise and in November 1791 he moved to a three-room apartment in Bank Street (now) in Dumfries. After receiving a 'burgess right' for the education of his children in Dumfries schools, he finally moved into a fine, red sandstone house in Burns Street (now), Dumfries. In January 1796, Burns fell seriously ill and was psychologically distressed over his finances. On 18 July that year he returned to Dumfries from Brow, a hamlet on the shores of the Solway Firth, where he was seeking a cure for his condition by sea-bathing. Merely four days after his return, he succumbed to his illness in Dumfries.

Burns had a brief life, but his early death at the age of 37 in the midst of his popularity drove people to the scenes associated with him, which were visited and grieved over. Upward of 20,000 people witnessed Burns' funeral procession when he was finally laid to rest amidst gun salutes in St Michael's Churchyard in Dumfries. Enthusiasts came to see the places and landscapes linked to the events of Burns' life. His enduring popularity during his life and after death led to the growth of visitors in the early 19th century to the places associated with him. Burns' birthplace and its environs were developed with more astonishing speed than any of his contemporaries (Watson, 2006).

Over the years, with the growing sense of Scottish national consciousness, Robert Burns has slowly metamorphosed from a Romantic poet into an iconic heritage. Robert Burns himself is an attraction and has emerged as a unique selling point of Scottish tourism and receives a mention in all forms of tourism literature. In Scotland, Robert Burns is the most copiously used cultural icon, surpassing his literary value to become a strong symbol of Scottish identity and is presented as a commodity for consumption to tourists. A government report in 2005 said Robert Burns is worth nearly £160 million to Scotland's economy (The Scottish Government News, 2005). Another report, 'The Burns Journey', prepared for Scottish Enterprise has identified 77 monuments (commemorative 'assets') relating to Burns spread throughout Scotland and furthermore proposed proper 'branding' of Burns as a product (Tourism Resources Company, 2006). This fact highlights his 'touristic' value. I will now look at how Robert Burns, despite being a cultural heritage, surpasses literary values to be transformed into an aesthetic tourism product. In the second section we will see how this 'touristification' or 'commodification' has impacted, if at all, on the 'authenticity' of the places associated with him.

The growth and spread of Robert Burns across Scotland might be attributed to the emerging quest of Scottish cultural identity. Simpson (1994: xvi) recognises this: 'Since the Union of 1707, Scots had felt the need to prove their right to cultural partnership with English. In Burns they found their great poet.' Furthermore, this was also reiterated by the language he chose to write. 'He wrote in the language of a sovereign Scotland almost two hundred years after the Union of Crowns of 1603' (McGuirk, 1994: 60–61). This may be seen through a nationalistic lens, as his writings bolstered the idea of Scottish nationhood. Robert Burns, in this sense, assumed a political role, as a legacy for the nationalistic fervour of the Scots to claim their authority over their past. Thus, place associated with Robert Burns also meant homage to the Scots to reiterate their sense of nationhood. This could be further understood from the fact that Burns' Night is almost a second national day, celebrated on 25 January with Burns suppers around the world, and much more widely observed than the official national day: St Andrew's Day. Lindsay (1994: 343) acknowledges this political and poetical appeal of Burns,

> Burns must therefore be considered a political as well as poetical figure, at any rate so far as Scotland is concerned. For his work more than the

> work of any other single person has kept Scotland in mind of her ancient nationhood, traditions and identity, throughout more than a century and a half of relentless buffeting towards that spiritual oblivion which total submersion in the culture and way of life of England or America must inevitably mean.

Burns' political role can be attributed to flexibility in the interpretation of his works. This malleability of Burns to be interpreted from a socialist perspective in the 20th century and credence to laissez-faire liberalism throughout the 19th century made it possible for him to be a figure that has been venerated for so long (Finlay, 1997). David McCrone (2001) reiterates this point and has concluded that the longevity of 'lad o' pairts' myth owes much to the fact that it can be appropriated for ideological use by both the left and the right, Unionists and Nationalists.

Burns' iconic stature was bolstered by this combination of poetic and political colours. 'Both popular appreciation and academic study of Burns have been coloured by the fact that Burns rapidly became a mythological figure, an icon' (Simpson, 1994: xv). McGuirk (1994: 55) considers Robert Burns to be the Elvis Presley of his time, in two senses,

> ...in the strong component of class-nostalgia in the foundation of his cult and in the way his icon, even during his life but increasingly after his death, was so often detached from his actual body of work. And if Burns was their Elvis Scotland was (with Switzerland) the Victorians' theme park, their Disney World.

It is inappropriate to compare Burns with Elvis, who represents a modern celebrity culture, but his popularity was immense by any standard of that time. 'Almost any scene connected with his birth, life or death became a shrine for literary tourists for whom, by 1851, "the one who does not visit them is considered deficient in taste"' (Gold & Gold, 1995: 64). Visitors thronging to the places of Burns' association transformed him from an iconic poet to a visitor attraction through the construction of monuments erected with an eye to attracting visitors, making people less interested in his poetry than in his legendary properties (Lindsay, 1994). Though this is not unarguable, what we can say is that there were more reasons than his literary skill for which people visited him. For example, Herbert (2003) assigns three motivating factors for Burns visitors: first, because of its 'connection with him', second, these places had the capacity to act as a catalyst of memoirs or hold an ideal or image, and third, because of important events that occurred in those places.

The subsequent result is that Robert Burns is now an important marker of Scottish cultural identity. The website of the World Burns Club (2008) notes,

> Robert Burns is one of the most famous characters in Scottish Cultural History. His importance is immense, not only in terms of his fascinating story and his work... but as a living tradition, carried from generation to generation throughout the World. Everyone, everywhere, who joins in the celebration of Scotland, Scottish Heritage or Scottish Culture, will witness references to Robert Burns.

None of the tourism literature on Scotland lacks mention of Robert Burns. 'He is omnipresent in our commercial iconography' (Noble, 1994: 167). Though there is no dearth of literature on the life and works of Robert Burns, his growth as a cultural commodity is not extensively pursued. But what is clearly visible is that in Scotland Robert Burns is not confined within his writings or literary circles but far more manifested as a tourism product. As a tourism destination, Scotland possesses an image and identity that bears allegiance to Robert Burns, which hardly any other single historical personality does anywhere else. An example of Robert Burns being a marketable brand can be observed from the fact that there is a hair salon by the name of Robert Burns in Dumfries, in the same house where, as an excise officer, he stayed for a brief period. The website of one of the pubs in Dumfries states, 'Established in 1610, The Globe Inn, Dumfries has long been associated with Robert Burns, Scotland's national poet' (The Globe Inn, 2008). Similarly, a guest house in Dumfries, the Ferintosh, promotes Dumfries and its historical ties to Robert Burns. It says 'we continue our tradition of hosting an Annual Burns Supper complete with piper, lavish spread of Scottish foods, and a whisky tasting contest'.

As a poet and songwriter, Burns' achievement was distinguished in his adeptness in writing words for existing music, and ability to range widely in terms of subject and mood (Simpson, 1994). The dialects in his songs and poems insist upon the separate and unique status and vocabulary of 'Scottishness' (McGuirk, 1994). Simpson (1994: xvi) believes, 'as a compensation for the loss of nationhood, Burns, allegedly epitomising Scottish characteristics, became a focus for national pride'.

Robert Burns has become significant in contemporary Scotland. Burns' place in Scotland's politics and identity is so immense that the opening of the Scottish Parliament on 1 July 1999 was marked by the rendition of a radical song by Burns. The importance of Burns to Scotland's tourism is made more visible by the Scottish Executive's decision to mark the year 2009 as Homecoming Scotland. Homecoming Scotland 2009 was a promotional drive to revive the Scottish economy, primarily through tourism, whilst commemorating the '250th anniversary of the birth of Scotland's national poet and cultural icon Robert Burns' (VisitScotland, 2009a). The event was launched to coincide with the anniversary of Burns' birthday on 25 January 2009 in Dumfries and Ayr by Scotland's first minister who also heads the Scottish Nationalist Party.

We will now look into some of the Burns-related museums in Ayrshire and Dumfriesshire.

Robert Burns House, Dumfriesshire

The Robert Burns House in Dumfries is the most prominent of the Burns sites in the region. Robert Burns lived the last few years of his life in this house and it exhibits 'Burns' items. To keep up with the practices prevalent in museums elsewhere, this museum maintains its strongly intact authenticity. About 50 metres of road approaching the Robert Burns House is paved stone and the façade of the house retains its 18th-century form. This, according to the curator, is to help the visitor sense the rural and pastoral atmosphere of Burns' time.

The ground floor of the museum has two rooms: the parlour, which is also used as an exhibition area and an information desk that sells Burns souvenirs, and the kitchen, with a scullery. The parlour displays some of Burns' manuscripts. Interestingly, amongst the manuscripts displayed here is one which is a copy rather than Burns' original manuscript (information provided by the custodian of the house in a personal communication). This duplicate manuscript remains displayed here without any notification. The first floor has two bedrooms, Burns' study room and the maid's bedroom. In his bedroom a box bed is exhibited. This bed does not correlate with a nearby drawing and description of Burns' actual bedroom which has no box bed. Other exhibits in the room include the tables and chairs. They are the representation of Burns' historical period rather than his possessions. Items in the exhibit also include a borrowed desk and chair from his friend's house where he had spent a few days, displayed in Burns' study room in a manner so as to make them look original.

The affirmation of authenticity is clarified by a leaflet, *The Story of Robert Burns House*, which states '(L)abels are kept to a minimum in Robert Burns House to make it as *authentic* as possible' (emphasis added). The museum also provides a free guided tour of Burns' mausoleum, which is a few minutes' walk away. The mausoleum itself is a replacement of Burns' original grave. The original grave, which lay about 50 feet west of the current mausoleum, was found inappropriate by Burns enthusiasts, who then raised sufficient funds globally to build the new mausoleum, completed in 1815, where his grave was later relocated (Watson, 2006).

Additionally, there is another heritage centre dedicated to Burns in Dumfries. The Robert Burns Centre is located on the other side of town, across the river Nith and has no connection with the poet as such. It was converted from an 18th century watermill and opened in 1986. The centre is a kind of multipurpose commercial structure, housing a movie theatre and a restaurant within. There is a small museum of Robert Burns in a portion of the first floor and a small reception/souvenir shop that sells Burns memorabilia. Visual images are utilised within the centre of the museum to show any connection with the poet and there are a few artefacts on display. The centre runs a small audio-visual presentation on Burns with a nominal charge of £1.60. Though named after Robert Burns, the centre shows limited focus on Burns and instead is a fine example of the use of the Robert Burns brand for the other commercial activity housed within.

Ellisland Farm, Dumfriesshire

About six miles away from Dumfries lies Ellisland Farm, which is another museum dedicated to Robert Burns. The poet moved to this farm in 1788 and spent some years of his life trying his luck at farming, without much success. The museum brochure, *Ellisland Farm, Home of Robert Burns 1788–1791*, asserts authenticity through its emphasis on the word 'original', it reads '(H)ere you can see some of Robert Burns' *original* writings and possessions. The kitchen has the *original* fireplace, oven and "swey"' (emphasis added). The brochure continues '(T)oday Ellisland provides a wonderful insight into Robert Burns' life and farming over *two hundred years ago*' (emphasis added). The brochure asks visitors to 'follow the footsteps of Burns…' an appeal to bring visitors virtually back to the time of Burns in an effort to connect visitors with the Scottish past. A video documentary, *Ellisland – An Honest Narrative*, is shown to visitors in which a reconstructed life of Burns in Ellisland is shown. The word *honest* stresses the authenticity of the narrative in the documentary.

Most artefacts presented in the farm are not Burns' own but are 'the sort of stuff he would use', states the museum curator (personal communication), although some of them, such as a sword, an arithmetic book, a tree trunk reworked by Burns, and song manuscripts, actually were Burns' own. The curator also believes that due to its location this farm is 'more original than other farms' and remains unchanged when compared with those not associated with the poet. The isolated location and rurality of Burns' heritage brings forth the idea of nationalism expressed by Bruce King, who has pointed out that, '(n)ationalism is an urban movement which identifies with the rural areas as a source of authenticity, finding in the "folk" the attitudes, beliefs, customs and language to create a sense of national unity among people who have other loyalties' (1980: 42). This view is further illustrated in the words of the curator at Ellisland, 'Robert Burns was different than other poets because he was original, honest, an humanitarian poet and song writer. He lifted Scotland by his pen being mightier than a sword. He boosted the morale of Scotland as a nation' (personal communication).

The Cottage, Alloway, Ayrshire

Alloway is near the town of Ayr, where William Burnes, father of Robert Burns, moved to from the north-east of Scotland in 1751 and where Robert Burns was born in 1759. The town is moderately bigger than Dumfries and lies in close proximity to Glasgow, Scotland's largest city. Unlike Dumfries, the town does not retain any of its medieval appearance and bears a much more modern look. It is a seaside town and receives significantly more tourists because of its location and proximity to nearby airports. Despite being host to Robert Burns' birthplace, the town does not seem to portray strongly any indication of this association. The middle of the town centre features a Burns statue in a square named after him. Approximately two miles from the town centre is Burns National Heritage Park, with Burns Cottage and Museum, Burns Monument and Gardens, Kirk Alloway, Auld Brig o'Doon and the Tam o'Shanter Experience. In this section I will look into artefacts presented at Burns Cottage, the place where Burns was born, with its collection of the poet's artefacts.

Burns Cottage is the house where Burns was born. The cottage looks medieval and has a thatched rooftop. The outer surrounding of the place is that of a typical old village house and suggests the character of the Burns family's first home. The cottage has four rooms, the barn, the byre, the north room and the kitchen. Much of the exhibition is presented in simulation, and artefacts are arranged and presented in order to show periodic authenticity. Every exhibit displays a written description confirming whether it is original or not and does not in any way try to portray them in an unfactual way. This is incredible; the poet spent only seven years of his early life here, but the cottage still does not try to manufacture something for its promotion or authenticity by any act of fabrication.

We have seen in an earlier section how Burns' house relies on limited levels (markers) to assert its authenticity. The cottage instead relies more on descriptions and levels (markers). A short description mentions that 'in 1993 the Cottage was extensively refurbished', and much of it has now, indeed, been rebuilt to make it 'more authentic' of the time (Watson, 2006). The rebuilt cottage exemplifies the setting of a working-class village house of Burns' time. It brings to life the inside of pastoral village dwellings of the average Scots of Burns' time. Every exhibit in the adjoining museum displays a written description confirming whether the exhibit is original or not.

There is a debate that authenticity 'is located not in the artefacts per se or in the models on which they are based but in the *methods* by which they were made – in a way of doing, which is a way of knowing, in a performance' (Kirshenblatt-Gimblett, 1998: 196, italics in original). This was illustrated in another museum attached to the cottage, which has now been moved to a new location. It contained a punch bowl gifted to the poet by his father-in-law which was described as a copy of the original held at the British Museum. The museum displayed a collection of manuscripts and various other artefacts relating to Burns. Strangely, the museum had a manuscript with musical notes transcribed and a description that read, 'an original sheet of music, with notes by Burns, used for James Johnson's "Scots Musical Museum"'. This is contradictory to the fact that Burns could not transcribe his music and always sought someone else to do it.

The cottage shows a ten-minute documentary *The Auld Cley Biggin*. It features the life and times of Burns in Alloway. Since the poet lived much of his young life here as a boy this place has less to show of original artefacts from the place. The documentary concludes with a sentence, 'but it was here that the flame of first poetic genius was kindled'. As the place of Burns' birth, the cottage relies strongly on its position as a sacrosanct place to affirm its claim to Burns. The claim of being a sacrosanct place is a powerful assertion of authenticity.

Robert Burns Birthplace Museum, Alloway, Ayrshire

The Burns Museum which was in the house adjacent to the cottage has now moved to a brand new museum dedicated to commemorating Burns' heritage in Alloway. The new museum is five-minutes' walk away from the cottage and was opened to the public in December 2010. It is more modern in appearance and presents the artefacts in a simulated setting and has made extensive use of modern technology, like computer animation, sound and light effects. The museum brings together over 5000 artefacts, original manuscripts and memorabilia.

The museum brochure declares, 'housing the world's most important collection of Robert Burns life and work in a bright and modern building, the museum displays include many of the bard's original manuscripts and personal belongings'. The exhibition is organised around four main themes, namely, 'identity', 'inspiration', 'fame' and 'creative works', to explore the many facets of the life and work of Robert Burns.

> 'Identity' considers the poet's family and relationships and how these influenced his life and works. It presents Burns as a brother, a friend, a lover, a husband and a father and features artefacts such as a fragment of his wife, Jean Armour's, wedding dress and a letter to his brother William. The 'Inspiration' section explores Burns' influences in the fields of 'nature', 'books and music', 'politics', 'love' and 'belief'; 'Fame' is devoted to his status as a global icon and charts the growth of a 'cult of Burns' in the aftermath of his death. In the fourth section entitled 'Creative works', where original manuscripts, including 'Scots Wha Hae' and 'Auld Lang Syne' are on display, visitors can also listen to readings of Burns' poems in listening pods. (History Today, 2010).

In the words of Nat Edwards, director of the Robert Burns Birthplace Museum (Figure 6.1), the aim of the museum is to:

> ... provide a modern and relevant interpretation of Burns that will intrigue visitors of all ages, whether they are lifelong Burns enthusiasts or completely new to his work. Here you will not just be able to read the manuscript of Tam o'Shanter, you can see the fireplace round which Burns first heard the stories that he turned into that poem, and you can look out the window and see that landscape, places like the Kirk Alloway and Brig o'Doon where the poem takes place. It gives you every facet of the man and his work. (History Today, 2010)

Figure 6.1 Robert Burns Birthplace Museum, Alloway

The new museum is children oriented, with many activities available to children. Most of the artefacts are presented in an educative form rather than an interpretive one. It extensively uses interactive multimedia features. The museum's nationalist intent is conspicuously visible in one of the interactive features in the museum. A kiosk lets visitors interact with the poet on the 'Burning Issues' of Scotland. Through the touch screen feature of the multimedia, users can interact on issues covering taxation, devolution, revolution, smuggling, emigration, and monarchy. I will illustrate here a typical debate on Scottish devolution presented in the multimedia,

> Panel moderator: Aha! The Burning Issue of Devolution! Is the union between Scotland and England a historical inevitability based on profoundly shared values? Or is it brutal colonialism, disguised as neighbourliness?

First panelist: Scotland – I mean, North Britain – and England are bound by more than geographical proximity! Their Union brings peace and harmony to our isles.

Second panelist: Scotland's been sold down the river by its old enemy! Although there are definite advantages to a political union, in practice this has kept Scotland poor – and crushes its culture to boot!

Panel moderator: A pair of provocative positions! But what does Robert Burns have to say? Choose the panelist, whose views you think most represent those of Robert Burns.
(It then asks the user to choose one of the above panelist. After one is chosen by the user, the multimedia proceeds further.)

Robert Burns: The English steel we could disdain, Secure in valour's station. But English gold has been our bane, such a parcel of rogues in a nation. Have I often said to myself, what are all the boasted advantages which my country reaps from a certain Union, that can counterbalance the annihilation of her independence, and ever her very name!
(The multimedia then signals that Burns' idea is close to that of the second panelist, who can be easily identified as a Scottish nationalist by his strong comment.)

Panel moderator: Mr Burns, you're clearly a patriotic Scot, but weren't you also a member of the Royal Dumfriesshire Volunteers – the force established to defend the Union's interest against the Scots' natural allies, the French!

Panel moderator again: And you, my friend? In two minds, when the choices are clear? Decisions! Decisions!
Burns was a patriot. But he also saw the merits of union in times of trouble – such as when France went on the rampage. Does this make Burns a '90 minute nationalist' or a defender of Scotland and its right to determine its own destiny? Perhaps you should decide where your loyalties lie! Surely it's time to come down off the fence when it comes to devolution?
And then, join me again soon in the hot seat for more ... Burning Issues!
(Monitor returns to homepage of Burning Issues again where the user can choose other issues.)

This example can be chosen as a mark of the increased nationalist sentiment in Scotland. The debate presented in the 'Burning Issues' kiosk is highly contextual in contemporary Scotland. It reiterates that Burns has uniform appeal across all political spectrums, but the way debate is presented in the museum makes a strong effort to present Burns more from the nationalists' side, which is meaningful.

The new birthplace museum charges a single entrance fee of £8.00 per adult. This also allows access to the cottage, which is a five-minute walk away. The total number of visitors to the museum was 444,947 in 2011, which is a huge 49.1% increase over the previous year (VisitScotland, 2011). Barely within two years of operation, the Robert Burns Birthplace Museum has become the fourth highest paid attraction in Scotland.

Burns Association as an attraction in Dumfries

Despite its strong connection with Burns, the town of Dumfries has not been successful in attracting as many tourists as it could by exploiting his name. However, most of the tourism attractions in the town centre are related to Burns and his associations. There is a walking trail designed to incorporate areas patronised by Burns named 'A Burns Trail, in the footsteps of Robert Burns.' The brochure *A Burns Trail* states: '(W)alk along the pedestrianised

High Street, its alignment virtually unchanged since medieval days'. The centre of the town has a statue dedicated to Burns, which was erected in 1882, and the High Street is a vehicle-free zone. Within this zone sits the Midsteeple, recently renovated, where the poet's body was kept until his final funeral procession which was attended by over 20,000 people. The entire stretch of the vehicle-free zone is paved. Additionally there are other places of the poet's patronage, most importantly, the poet's favourite 'howff', The Globe Inn, that 'with its close retains much of its former atmosphere'. Established in 1610, The Globe Inn has long been associated with Robert Burns. Its website states that, in 1796 Burns wrote: '... the Globe Tavern here, which these many years has been my Howff...' and that in 1819, the first of what was to become the annual tradition of Burns Suppers was held here (The Globe Inn, 2011). His favourite seat still survives here, and some of his poetry may still be seen inscribed by Robert Burns with a diamond on his bedroom windows. Through the middle of the town flows the river Nith, which is spanned by a 13th-century bridge, now reserved only for pedestrians. Beside it is a seasonal museum, the 'Old Bridge House'. A statue dedicated to Burns' wife is placed in front of St Michael's Church, which houses his mausoleum.

What Meaning Can We Draw From These Examples of Authenticity?

The concept of authenticity is itself loose, and often difficulty arises in the question of how to ascertain what is authentic and what is not. Authenticity is often viewed as a dialectic and is endlessly constructed (Lowenthal, 2005). Though Jamal and Hill (2004) have suggested a framework for developing indicators of authenticity under the three dimensions – objective, constructed and personal – it is difficult to do so because, according to Richter (1999), it is often the politics of power which not only controls whose interpretation and definition of authenticity prevails but also what will be saved or remembered at all.

Authenticity in the case of a museum is also found to be negotiated in the external political environment (Chhabra, 2008). The fluidity of the concept of authenticity brings the dilemma of how to assign authentication to anything. Culler (1988) identifies this. The use of markers is a dilemma of authenticity because to be experienced as authentic it must be marked as authentic, but when it is marked as authentic it is mediated, a sign of itself, and hence lacks the authenticity of what is truly unspoiled, untouched by mediating cultural codes (Culler, 1988). Despite divergent views on how to classify authenticity there is a common agreement amongst both academicians and practitioners that authenticity assumes a central role in tourism and more often in the case of museums (Chhabra, 2008).

A common theme which all three museums of Burns share is that of the rural, pastoral life of Burns. This conveys two important messages. First, it gives visitors a sense of the social class Burns comes from, and second, the literary genre he represents: both of which are closely related in this case. Gold and Gold (1995: 63) associate Burns with the pastoral genre which represents the view of life and nature as seen from the standpoint of the common man rather than the lofty position of an aristocrat. Burns' view of landscape was more akin to that of the tenant farmer, having 'the eye of one who knows hard labour, can appreciate prosperity and productivity' (Drabble 1979: 66, cited in Gold & Gold, 1995). Burns came from the rural class and his poems present a pastoral image. This portrayal of rurality is a potent identifier of a nation as Brennan (1990: 53) believes that the 'folk', the 'plebeians', the 'people', the 'working class' are important components of any inclusive treatment of a nation.

Furthermore, the idea of asserting authenticity in the Robert Burns museums appeals not only to the tourists but also to nationalists. A central aspect of the culture of modernity is the quest for an authentic experience (Mellinger, 1994). Tourism, which emerged with this modern search for authenticity, largely relies on the belief that authentic experiences reside outside the realm of everyday life in contemporary society (MacCannell, 1999; Urry, 2006). In a similar vein, 'continuity with a suitable historic past' is what Hobsbawm (1983: 1) believes every nation attempts to establish to assert its national significance. In this attempt the nation may seek to go for the 'invention of tradition', the tradition which helps them to assert being 'ancient, original and distinctive' (Trevor-Roper, 1983). These ideas coincide with tourists' interest in any destination, as proposed by MacCannell (1999), for whom tourism is synonymous with authenticity. He states, '(R)eality and authenticity are thought to be elsewhere: in other historical periods and other cultures, in purer, simpler lifestyles', and tourists often go in search of 'unspoiled natives' surrounded by landscape of pristine beauty (van den Berghe & Keyes, 1984: 346), seeking the exotic, primitive and natural elsewhere (Cohen, 1988; MacCannell, 1999).

What can be understood from the above is tourists' quest for authenticity, which helps make tourism represent an alter ego of national identity, as both nationalism and tourism strive towards representations of authentic national culture. Tourism, through these authentic representations, aids the ideals of nationalists in gaining 'cultural authenticity and unity' (Smith,

1991: 16). Burns' authenticity in this case signifies Scotland's authenticity as a nation because Burns is an important, strong marker in Scotland's national iconography.

The stories presented in these museums are an attempt to present Scotland's national identity as 'primordial, essential, unified and continuous' (McCrone, 2002: 264–265). McCrone (2002) writes that the 'past' is a powerful source of legitimacy for those who would change the present for a new future. According to him, the 'narrative' of the nation is told and retold through national histories, literatures, the media and popular culture, which together provide a set of stories, images, landscapes, scenarios, historical events, national symbols and rituals. Burns is a strong marker to assert Scotland's past not only because he signifies the nation's past but also because through his writing he claimed 'sovereign Scotland almost two hundred years after the Union of Crowns of 1603' (McGuirk, 1994: 60–61). This affirmation of Scotland's past in Burns transmits an important message because 'identification with a national past often serves as an assurance of worth against subjugation or bolsters a new sovereignty' (Lowenthal, 2005: 44).

The celebration of Homecoming Scotland in 2009 as a mark of Robert Burns' 250th birthday was a meaningful strategy, considering the fact that the Scottish Nationalist government at one point said it wanted to launch its Independence Referendum Bill on Burns' birthday (*The Scotsman*, 2008) (Figure 6.2). Through the name of Burns, it can be assumed that the incumbent Nationalist government hopes to achieve favourable political mileage. We know that homeland sentiment has been a favourite of poets and lyricists

Figure 6.2 Burns' Day celebration at Burns Mausoleum in Dumfries

(Connor, 2001). Burns is particularly popular with emigrants from Scotland, among whom his poetry evokes sentimental nostalgia about the Scotland their ancestors left behind, and with Scots, to whom he was an icon of Scottish nationalism (Grenier, 2005: 83). As Renan puts it '(A) heroic past, great men, glory (by which I understand genuine glory), this is the social capital upon which one bases a national idea' (Renan, 1990: 19).

Conclusions

This chapter has examined the interactions of tourism and cultural heritage on a common platform of authenticity. Whilst we should always be cautious of 'heritage' (Hewison, 1987), the authenticity of the touristic heritage of Burns gives a strong cultural identity to the region as he has a distinctive role in Scottish national identity. Burns is an icon not only for tourists but also to nationalists, because his heritage meets the various ideals of nationalism: where nation is imagined through cultural fragments, idealised with the sense of rurality, and legitimised with the assertion of authentic past: largely conforming to what Reicher and Hopkins (2001) argue in *Self and Nation*: that the goal of nationalists is to create an 'essentialised' sense of nation out of cultural fragments (cf. McCrone, 2001: 177).

The three museums examined in this chapter rely on the actual setting of the period of Burns and original artefacts which present authenticity. It presents Burns in a 'historic time' (Kirshenblatt-Gimblett, 1998) to the visitors. This means that most of the things in the museum are in fact presented in an 18th-century context, to represent the time period when Burns actually lived. There are also instances where fake or unoriginal artefacts are used to assert the authenticity of Burns and his association with the museum. This shows us that the ideal of Burns is more important than his artefacts. He has symbolic value rather than any actual or original belongings or artefacts alone. Berghoff and Korte (2002) believe that industrial heritage gained cultural and touristic significance because it had formed the basis of Britain's former industrial glory and therefore symbolises the country itself and a heroic epoch of its history. Burns represents Scotland's cultural distinctiveness and can be seen in a similar symbolic way in Scotland.

The idea of modernity implies that authenticity exists only in the past and helps preserve its signs, which are also important resources for nationalists (Culler, 1988). As Burns' artefacts are presented as being authentic, the Burns museums in the south-west of Scotland attempt to show Scotland as primordial, ancient, original and distinctive. Burns' role in contemporary Scotland reiterates his importance and shows his relevance as being more than just a poet. He is an icon who has universal appeal and is capable of instilling a sense of pride amongst fellow compatriots. The presentation of artefacts in the museums which are reproductions or unoriginal, the use of words in the brochures which are an assertion of the past, and the restoration efforts in the town of Dumfries are some examples that I have taken to show how authentic past is narrated to visitors in these sites. The narration of authenticity in Burns heritage sites serves as a strong testimony to Scotland's cultural distinctiveness – an act that directly converges with the ideals of nationalists whose aim, as has been noted previously, is to gain 'cultural authenticity and unity'. The past, according to Lowenthal (2005) is integral to a sense of identity. The authenticity shown in the three Burns museums conveys messages about the rurality and primordiality of Scotland which are important in presenting an authentic sense of the past.

It cannot be denied that tourists themselves are agents of multiple and even contradictory interpretations of sites and heritage. The guardians of the various sites are committed to directing and influencing these touristic constructions as much as possible in the name of good history, family loyalty and local fidelity (Fawcett & Cormack, 2001). The important segment of visitors who come to visit Scotland because of their strong sense of history and family loyalty are the ones who have their familial ties with Scotland. They are visitors of Scottish descent who come to Scotland because they believe it is where their roots are, for which they have a great affection. We have also observed in this chapter that the anniversary of Burns' birth in 2009 was marked by celebrating Homecoming Scotland. In the next chapter, we will see how genealogical tourists to Scotland associate themselves with their ancient nation and whether the celebration of events like homecoming can be meaningful from a nationalistic perspective.

7 Genealogical Tourists and Homeland Nationalism

Introduction

In 2009 Scotland marked 'Homecoming Scotland', celebrating some of the country's great contributions to the world, such as golf, whisky, great Scottish minds and innovations, and Scotland's rich culture and heritage. The campaign was aimed at persuading genealogical tourists from around the world to visit Scotland, particularly from countries with large Scots diaspora populations, such as Canada, the United States, Australia and New Zealand, and other parts of the United Kingdom. In this chapter I will delve into genealogical tourists, their feelings about their home nation and how that corresponds with the sense of Scottish nationalism. It shows that travel to one's ancestral land bestows a renewed sense of self-identity, enhances cultural affinity to the visitor's 'homeland' nation and also plays a role in articulating 'homeland' nationalism. We will finally note that such celebrations carry forward an underlying message that is in tune with the nationalist agenda.

The importance of Scottish diaspora communities in the development of Scottish national feeling cannot be exaggerated; Scotland is a country of emigrants (McCrone, 2001: 70) that has a long history of outward migration. There are many reasons for this migration: prominent among them are the Highland Clearances and the expansion of the British colonies. The result of this outward migration has been a considerable spread of people of Scottish descent all over the world and most visibly in the former dominions of the British colonies and in the United States and Canada. The Scottish Parliament has recently identified this as an important market for Scottish tourism (Basu, 2007). Following this, the Scottish tourism agency has initiated various measures to encourage people of Scottish descent to travel back to their ancestral land.

Many scholars have agreed that touring an ancestral land is different from the experience of general heritage visitors because genealogical tourists also bring in different levels of personal and emotive connections to places and artefacts (Stephenson, 2002; Timothy, 1997, 2008; Timothy & Boyd, 2003). Often such experience is related to personal enrichment and gives the visitors a sense of being 'at home' (Stephenson, 2004: 62). In this chapter I will explore how this enrichment can be related to the idea of nationalism and how tourists with Scottish ancestral roots identify themselves with Scotland. My argument until now has been that as a medium to promote one's culture and national identity, tourism is an expression of nationalism. In the following paragraphs I will extend this argument to show that genealogical tourism is another way to advance nationalist sentiment by offering an experience that reinforces the common cultural affinity of the tourists to their ancestral land.

Genealogical tourism is considered to be one of the fastest growing sub-segments of the heritage market (Santos & Yan, 2010). However, scholars have largely overlooked this area of research until very recently. Though some researchers have slowly started to show some interest in the touristic value of this segment of tourists, it is still at a very early stage (see Coles & Timothy, 2004b). This is evident in the fact that different terminology is used while dealing with this sub-segment of heritage tourism; for example, it is often referred to as personal heritage (Timothy, 1997), roots tourism (Basu, 2007; Wright, 2009), legacy tourism (McCain & Ray, 2003), genealogical tourism (Santos & Yan, 2010), diasporic tourism (Leite, 2005), ethnic tourism (King, 1994), or ancestral tourism (Fowler, 2003).

However, the central feature of genealogical tourism is that it is premised on embracing 'commonness'. It contrasts with other forms of tourism, which is fundamentally the 'industry of difference' (Hollinshead, 1998): that is, travellers come to visit and know new and interesting people and pasts. In opposition to that popular notion, the aspiration of roots tourists is the search for familiarisation and identification with others (Stephenson, 2004: 74). Thus, the voyage of the genealogical tourist is to find affinity and commonness; and rather than travelling away from home these tourists are travelling to their 'home'. In this chapter we will see how the realisation of this commonness binds tourists emotionally to the ancestral land and bestows a renewed sense of self-identity and cultural affinity to their homeland.

Diasporas and Nationalism

As with diasporic tourists, the role of diasporas and other transnational activities in the development of nationalism has been explored very little.

Many scholars have termed it 'long-distance nationalism' or 'homeland nationalism' (Anderson, 1992; Brubaker, 1996; Schiller & Fouron, 2002). Their idea is that long-distance nationalism brings together those who share a sense of 'peoplehood' based on common culture and history by situating people in their ancestral homeland. Importantly long-distance nationalism cannot be seen as 'top-down', but springs from the life experiences of migrants whose lives extend across borders.

The life experience of an individual is largely informed by one's ethnicity, which also forms an important basis of ethnic nationalism (Nash, 2002). Smith (1991) separates nationalism into two distinct kinds: territorial or civic, and ethnic nationalism. According to him, in a western, civic model national unity arises from a historic territory, laws and institutions, the legal political equality of members that expresses itself in a set of rights and duties, and a common civic culture and ideology. A non-western ethnic nation is based on descent or presumed descent, and thus is seen by its members as a 'fictive super-family' (Shulman, 2002: 556). Most commonly, the western version of nationalism is defined as civic and the eastern version as ethnic, though, there is an Irish exception to this. Irish nationalism is an example of the ethnic type, despite being located in the west. Smith (1991: 13) acknowledges that every nationalism contains civic and ethnic elements in varying degrees and in different forms. In the case of Scotland, its nationalism is considered as the civic type. But this view has been contested by Hearn (2000), who is sceptical of the claim that nationalism in Scotland is indeed purely 'civic' (cf. McCrone, 2001). The ethnic element in Scottish nationalism is shown by the importance given to ancestry as a marker of 'being Scottish' (McCrone, 2001). McCrone notes that in answer to a question about putative Scottish citizenship, indicating the value of ethnicity in determining Scottishness, a total of 73% of people in Scotland believe ancestry is important.

Diasporas can play an important role in the development of nationalism (Carter, 2004; Mulligan, 2002). In Scotland, they bear an additional significance because Scottish emigration is marked by two historical trends: first, the loss of its independence 300 years ago; and second, relative deprivation and underdevelopment in comparison to England. Many diasporic groups reside and function in a host country but retain strong emotional and allegiance connections to their countries of origin (Kelly, 2000; Sheffer, 1986, cited in Timothy, 2008). This emotional bonding with their homeland opens immense opportunities for governments back home. Schiller and Fouron (2002: 357) note that an 'increasing number of states are developing legal ways of reclaiming emigrants and their descendants'. China and India have seen unprecedented return investment by their diasporic communities for the economic development of their countries. They can also be useful politically.

An example is Croatia, where the government encouraged visits by diasporic Croatians as a way of garnering support for independence from Yugoslavia and these tourists were encouraged to play several important political roles (Carter, 2004). Additionally, the Irish case of Homecoming also shows that the promotional drive geared towards diasporas cannot be free from political and cultural agendas (Morgan *et al.*, 2002). Morgan and Pritchard (2004), in their observation of 'Irish Homecoming', note that a tourism campaign aimed at Welsh diasporas was biased in its representation of Wales in its promotion and believed political definitions of place were used to 'construct' Wales. According to them, 'Welsh Wales' was marginalised in the campaign and 'British Wales' or the metropolitan view from Cardiff, which they argue is rootless, placeless and lacking the vibrancy of 'Welsh' Wales, were promoted in order to conform with the dominant message of devolved Welsh governance (Morgan *et al.*, 2002).

There are closer examples to show us that the importance of nation, understood as cultural community, extends beyond territorial borders. Scottish diasporas have been actively appropriating a Scottish identity in their adopted country, and particularly in the United States, which has officially designated 6 April as Tartan Day, commemorating the Declaration of Arbroath, the Scottish declaration of independence signed on 6 April 1320 (Hague, 2002). Basu (2007: 19) notes that 'the most powerful expression of diasporic idealisation of the Scottish homeland is the 1995 feature film, *Braveheart*, a classic example of romantic nationalist obfuscation that must be understood as both product and partial cause of the Scottish heritage revival'. Cultural identity shared between people beyond national borders can bring camaraderie, attuned towards a collective cultural aspiration with the homeland.

The south-west region has witnessed the biggest displacement of the Scottish population, owing to various factors (Aitchison & Cassell, 2003). Though the Scottish Highlands loom large in the popular story of Scottish emigration, scholars agree that it was a phenomenon across the board in Scotland (Devine, 2000; Donaldson, 1966). Devine (2000), who has examined the causes of Scottish emigration in the three regions of the Highlands, the agricultural lowlands and urban industrial areas, concludes that Lowland emigration was more to do with the lure of opportunity than destitution and deprivation. Canada was the great magnet for those who wished to work the land, while rural tradesmen and industrial workers tended to opt more for the United States. However, because of a popular perception of Scotland as the country of the Highlands, tourism and genealogical research have both drawn attention to those areas and the region of the south-west is largely neglected. Though an account of genealogical heritage and its relation with tourism in the Scottish Highlands has been looked into by Basu (2007) in his anthropological account, no such work has been done in the region of the south-west of Scotland, which is why I have chosen to study the genealogical travellers to the south-west region.

Homeland and Self-Identity

The concept of home and homeland seems to be associated with the presence of family, together with some aspect of 'belonging' to the nation or culture (Hughes & Allen, 2010). It has different effects on individuals' identity. There are many reasons for people to travel to their homeland – one of them being the search for 'ancestry' (Wright, 2009). It brings 'consciousness of myths, nostalgia, imagined and actual histories of the group' (Coles & Timothy, 2004a: 13) and functions as a means to 'renew, reiterate and solidify familial and social networks' (Duval, 2004: 51). In their study of Irish emigrants to the United Kingdom, Hughes and Allen (2010) find that a desire to visit was expressed by some older informants as an opportunity to recapture childhood memories and in that sense Ireland was interpreted as 'home' – a place of origin. For some the visit stimulated a sense of Irishness.

The potency of a genealogical visit lies in the fact that it can bring the hitherto unconscious sense of Scottishness to the fore where a diasporic tourist is concerned. Realising this, the Scottish tourist agency tries to capture the appeal of 'home' to the diasporas. A website dedicated to genealogical visitors states,

> Scotland is a land of five million people. A proud people, passionate about their country and her rich, noble heritage. For every single Scot in their native land, there are thought to be at least five more overseas who can claim Scottish ancestry – that's many, many millions spread throughout the globe. For them, for you, Scotland is *home*. And, of course, there's no place like it. A trip to Scotland – a trip back home – is surely the best way to feel connected to this ancient land. A way to feel part of something greater than the here and now. A way to truly belong. (Ancestral Scotland, 2010; emphasis added)

Scholars have noticed that genealogical tourism has the propensity to enhance one's root identity (Basu, 2004; Leite, 2005). Basu (2004) notes that in Scotland tours organised for genealogical tourists are meaningfully designed to help them identify themselves with the artefacts and landscapes of their ancestry to enhance their Scottish root identity. This is done at two levels. At the local level, according to Basu (2004), geographical tools, such as clan maps and family museums, together with tours that highlight the hillocks, streams, valleys, and fields known to one's ancestors, are often utilised by 'roots' destinations to enhance a sense of belonging to the land, thereby creating a sense of solidarity as people re-root their identities with others who inhabit or have inhabited these 'sacred places' (cf. Timothy, 2008). At the promotional level, the national tourism agency instils a sense of Scottishness. A good example is the Scottish tourism agency, which tries to capture this in its website Ancestral Scotland, by giving the following answer to its question: what does it mean to be Scottish?:

> Many people would say that it is to do with the heart and not the head; a feeling that cannot be simply rationalised. Some would describe it as a sense of connection with Scotland and an acute awareness that Scotland is a place that can be truly described as *'home'*. *Homecomers* – people who have travelled sometimes huge distances to visit an ancestral farmstead or lay flowers on the grave of an ancestor – talk movingly of the experience. They often find it difficult to put into words but there is a strong feeling of self-knowledge and self-worth while at the same time they talk of a powerful association with a place and its people.
>
> That sense of connection is felt, too, by people who have never left their *native* Scotland. Pride in their birthplace, pride in a unique heritage and pride in the global community of people of Scottish ancestry. We may all be, as the Scots dialect puts it 'a fine mixter-maxter', but we are all Scottish and proud of it. (Ancestral Scotland, 2010; emphasis added)

The above example shows an attempt directed towards bringing people closer to their ancestral land and tries to remind them where they belong and where their roots are. Through the use of the words 'home' and 'native', the Ancestral Scotland website tries to capture the element of connection that binds diasporas to their land. Billig (2001: 75) has looked into how a nation is daily reminded of nationhood by the use of words, 'we', 'us', 'our': homeland is imagined as unity, in a way 'it is the place of "our" personal homes – my home, your home – and, as such, it is the home of all of "us", the home of the homes, the place where all of "us" are at home'. A survey of genealogical visitors was carried out to see how they feel about their travel to Scotland. Their views confirm that a strong emotional attachment exists between diasporas and their 'native' land and that travel to their ancestral land is instrumental to their self-identity and cultural affinity. The survey reveals three themes: (i) a belonging to the 'ancestral' nation, (ii) finding roots and discovering Scottishness, and (iii) identifying with Scotland's future.

Belonging to the 'ancestral' nation

In his seminal *The Symbolic Construction of Community*, A.P. Cohen (1985a) argues that the reality of community lies in its members' perception of the vitality of its culture. He believes that people construct community symbolically, making it a resource and a repository of meaning, and a referent of their identity. Respondents feel strongly they belong to the Scottish nation as a cultural community. 'Nation' in this sense can be referred to as a community of the same cultural affinity. The following responses provide a useful tool to see the diasporic movement to homeland as a journey to their own nation:

> ... Many are curious about their roots and would like to know more about the homelands of their forefathers and locate any current relatives... Most with roots in Scotland are proud of their native country and the people who still live there. (American male over 60 years old)

> ... I feel exalted when I visit Scotland. I have visited here several times and each visit gives me a new insight into my own identity and my nativeness. I practice my Scottish roots in New Zealand and celebrate Burns' day, Hogmanay, enjoy Burns' supper and haggis... I feel Scots communities abroad are more Scottish than people here in Scotland. (New Zealand male over 45 years old)

> ... knowing my roots gives me more of a sense of where I belong in the world as a whole. It also explains the origin of many customs, characteristics and mannerisms within my family, e.g. thriftiness, self-reliance, independence of thought, music and dancing... My study of my own genealogy has shown me from where many of these characteristics and mannerisms derive, and why they are to be cherished and not denied. Knowledge of my Scots descent also grounds me in the geopolitics of today's world. My studies have shown me the roots of troubles in Ireland, the impact that English imperialism has caused all over the world. I'm very proud of my Scots roots. I only wish that Scotland and Wales could be free and independent, that Ireland could be united... (American male over 60 years old)

The respondents also express their desire to return. Williams and Hall (2000) and Duval (2002) have shown that the diasporic movement can potentially lead to return migration. In the case of Croatia, the government set about making return more attractive and was able to encourage return migration of 1000 people from the United States (Carter, 2004). The following responses testify to the respondents' desire for return, arising out of their visits to Scotland:

> My youngest son has asked many times that we move to Scotland (he wants us to buy a castle and convert it into a 'bed and breakfast') – not an unreasonable idea, but I am a bit too old to be starting such an adventure – maybe he will. (American male over 60 years old)

> I learned about my Scottish roots in 1987, joined the Stewart Society of Edinburgh in 1988 and made my first visit to Scotland in 1989. I have tried to return every year, and intend to visit all parts of the country. (American male over 60 years old)

Leite (2005) uses the term *imaginative reconstruction* to describe diasporic yearnings to relive the past. It is through this reconstruction that tourists engage, not merely sensing the past or reliving ancestral experience in the present, but actually imagining themselves 'there and then'. She says experiential commemoration can produce powerful emotional effects that make tourists experience a 'return' to the homeland that has been lost. This is evident in the responses from tourists in the following way,

> I felt I'd 'come home'... I'm staying in a house only 2 doors away from where my granddad lived before emigrating. That gives me a huge buzz. I have photos of ancestors' tombstones and of homes in which they lived. I get a huge emotional thrill from seeing the houses & hills & rivers they saw. My Scottishness, always there even as a child, is now a very real and important part of me. (New Zealand female over 60 years old)

> ... I will always be drawn to Scotland at heart level, and love the culture, history and colour of the country. There's a part of me that will always be Scottish... So it's the sentimental, the nostalgic, the past that attracts me. (Australian female over 60 years old)

To the genealogical visitors, visiting their ancestral land is reliving the past of their ancestors. It is a way to reconnect them emotionally with their land. The land for them is native land, where they belong. This act of reliving their past strengthens their authentic self and nativeness.

Finding roots and discovering Scottishness

A visit to the homeland is akin to a spiritual quest and a search for meaning in the lives of the people of the diaspora (Lowanthal, 1985). Wang's

(1999) idea of existential authenticity helps us explain this. He characterises the ideal of authenticity by either nostalgia or romanticism. According to Wang, it is nostalgic because it idealises the ways of life in which people are supposed to be freer, more innocent, more spontaneous, purer and truer to themselves than usual – such ways of life are usually supposed to exist in the past or in childhood. It is also romantic because it accents the naturalness, sentiments and feelings in response to the increasing self-constraints of reason and rationality in modernity. In this way, tourists, according to Wang, are in search of their authentic selves with the aid of activities or toured objects. The search for roots by visits to 'home' by the people of the diaspora is strongly characterised by this. Braziel and Mannur (2003) note that notions of home, identity and exile are also accompanied by the propensity to prioritise the geographical, political, cultural and subjective spaces of the home nation as an authentic space of belonging: this constantly appears in the responses in this chapter.

The respondents in this study viewed their travel to Scotland as importantly linked to their desire to find their roots and that the journey was instrumental in enriching their Scottishness. A number of them said the consciousness of their Scottish roots, realised by their visit to those places, would now be another feature of their personal identity. They feel that Scottishness is more strongly embedded since their visit than before. The following examples are typical:

> There is an important sense of identity with the name Johnston and Scotland (Kirkudbrightshire) – this is reinforced with ancient ancestry… which provides identity further back. Being of proven Scottish descent provides a sense of where I come from, and a link to all that is Scottish culture. (Canadian male over 45 years old)

> …there is much in my homeland to reinforce that Scottish identity. I spent time in researching my husband's family…Again mostly Scottish background…and this was new for them. I think that a stronger connection to their roots will result from this research. (Canadian female over 60 years old)

Genealogical tourism provides a platform where visitors can reinforce historic memories through visits to commemorative sites because tourists and package tours mostly focus on visiting public monuments, cultural centres and representative landscapes (Leite, 2005). Leite further believes that commemorative practices somatically and imaginatively unite them with their forebears, and bridge the diasporic rupture of past and present, ancestors and selves, homeland and exile. These practices also help in conferring an identity to the diasporic travellers because 'histories of ancestors or mythological events become an intimate part of their present identity' in Scotland (McCrone *et al.*, 1995: 181). These visits make tourism to the ancestral land an opportunity to encounter hitherto heard and unheard histories. A personal visit gives them a sense of reality or a feeling of authenticity. Rather than imagining the country through fables or home legends, the visit materialises a real meaning of being Scottish and a real sense of authentic Scottishness. A respondent confirms this by saying that 'visits to real places in Scotland such as farms, towns, parishes, churchyards reinforce the reality or fact of Scottish origin, rather than relying on family legend or similar'.

Another respondent states:

> Visiting Scotland, especially the fortifications of my ancestors in the Borders, and reading about those times, gives me a sense of what their lives were like, especially during the times of the Border wars when England and Scotland were defining themselves as countries. Visiting the sites makes their history so very 'real', and not just names and dates. And travelling further north, into the Highlands, one is struck by the stunning beauty of the place, and how this people has endured both the travails of nature and man. Every time I visit the place, I love it more and more. I really enjoy the fact that, when I read about the places associated with my family's history – the structures, the battles, and the events, religious movements (Covenanters) – I can make a personal connection... it makes me part of it. (American male over 60 years old)

These examples reveal a sense of cultural unification because respondents feel more connected with Scottish identity after their visit. The cultural sense of being Scottish has indirect overtones to political nationalism (McCrone *et al.*, 1995), partly because cultural identity and national identity are inextricably linked in Scotland. For example, Scottish cultural icons like Robert Burns and Robert the Bruce have been serving interchangeably as cultural and national identities and often used for nationalistic purposes (Edensor, 1997a, 1997b).

Identifying with Scotland's future

Not all diasporas are identical. According to Timothy and Coles (2004) all diasporas are different and reflect the specificities of their conditions, histories, new homeland immigration policies and population sizes. Diasporas' views of Scotland are saturated with the historical images of

Scotland. History, heritage and landscape form the popular image of Scotland for the respondents in this chapter. But Scotland's history also brings with it its contemporary aspirations to become a fully independent nation-state, the political debate and constitutional status of Scotland within the United Kingdom and the desire for full independence. They all find a place in respondents' views. The disaporic tourists were informed by the debate over Scotland's aspiration for regaining full independence from the United Kingdom. Some of the respondents were more forthcoming in supporting Scottish independence:

> ... Gosh, it will be nice. You know I am surprised that Scotland is still part of the UK. I am looking forward to it ... (American male over 45 years old)
>
> Probably more of geography than history ... but the contribution of Scotland to the world is important ... if it would go for Independence it wouldn't surprise me, it wouldn't shock me and I wouldn't mind. (Canadian male over 60 years old)
>
> ... I have followed the modest attempts of Scotland to regain its independence with the reestablishment of the Scots Parliament and 'devolution', and was absolutely astounded with the defeat of the proposition of Scottish independence, until I learned that the vote was 'rigged' – those not voting all were 'counted' as votes against (more English chicanery) ... I really wish Scotland, as well as the Welsh, could be free and independent, and that Ireland would be united ... I only wish the Scots had taken the same path as the Irish in 1919 – Scotland may eventually get her freedoms and independence, but by then the Scottish North Sea oil will have been depleted ... I support Scottish independence. (American male over 60 years old).

However a different apolitical view was also evident. A respondent stated:

> Members of the Scottish diaspora do not necessarily relate to current politics in Scotland. Devolution and the possible separation of Scotland from the United Kingdom actually conflict with the Scotland which many abroad have envisioned. Personally I would prefer not to be involved in the political motivations of a modern Scotland. My ancestors lived in a different time and climate and I have spent time trying to conceptualise and understand that time period. Theirs was a far different world from modern Scotland. My interest has been history and not current politics and economic development. (American male over 60 years old).

The above views conform to an earlier study by Sim and Leith (2013) who found that half of the Scottish diasporic tourists they surveyed had some knowledge of Scottish current affairs and were aware of changes taking place within the country. These responses show that diasporic tourists have a unique bond with Scotland. Their visits to their ancestral land have a direct meaning for who they think they are and it enriches and reinforces their identity. It brings them closer to Scotland and its culture, and its contemporary aspirations. The three distinctive themes that emerge in the travel of the disapora, (i) belonging to the 'ancestral' nation, (ii) finding roots and discovering Scottishness and (iii) identifying with Scotland's future, strongly resonate with the ideals of nationalists. Against such a backdrop, any programme to entice diasporas to Scotland has a capacity to indirectly disseminate the enshrined message of nationalism. The celebration of events that are aimed at diasporas can be meaningful in one sense because such events help forge stronger ties with the home nation and its culture.

Homecoming Celebrations and National Objective

After organising the Homecoming Scotland 2009 celebration during the Scottish Nationalist Party's first term in office and in the Scottish Parliament, Scotland's First Minister Alex Salmond announced a plan to celebrate a second Homecoming in 2014 to commemorate the Scottish nationalists' hero King Robert the Bruce. Coinciding with the planned second Homecoming, he has also announced that the referendum on Scottish independence will be staged in September 2014 – the year that marks the 700th anniversary of the battle of Bannockburn. While making this announcement Salmond said,

> In 2014 the eyes of the world will be on Scotland as the Commonwealth Games comes to Glasgow and the Gleneagles hosts the Ryder Cup and Scots at home and abroad mark the anniversary of Bannockburn ... In this year of celebration, repeating the remarkable success and benefits of Homecoming 2009 is an excellent opportunity to attract tourism and investment and showcase the very best of Scotland. (The Scottish Government, 2010)

The date of the first celebration was very important because it commemorated Robert Burns' 250th anniversary. It commenced on the day of Burns' anniversary in January 2009, running through to St Andrew's Day on 30 November. We have observed in an earlier chapter that Burns' image invokes a nationalistic sentiment and use of his image in tourism is meaningful.

Severin Carrell (2012) takes the view that the year 2014 has also been deliberately chosen, as it is a year with considerable significance and resonance during which Scotland will be the focus of several major global sporting and cultural events. It is also a year that has particular resonance for hard-line nationalists: 2014 is the 700th anniversary of the Battle of Bannockburn and the date will embolden many nationalist activists (Carrell, 2012). There has also been a suggestion that a third such event could take place in 2020, to celebrate the 700th anniversary of the Declaration of Arbroath (Sim & Leith, 2013).

The overall objective of Homecoming 2009 was to deliver £44 million of additional tourism revenue to the country (VisitScotland, 2009a, 2009b). It was a moderately successful event when we consider a post-event evaluation that revealed it brought 72,000 additional tourists to Scotland and the net additional expenditure which they generated was £53.7 million (Ekos, 2010). However, using evocative icons for such celebrations cannot be regarded as appropriate when we take into account that English tourists occupy an important place in Scottish tourism, comprising 39.2% of the total tourists to Scotland. Against that backdrop, using Burns, or the more 'belligerent' Bruce or Bannockburn, when promoting Scotland through Homecoming cannot be wise from a marketing point of view. In fact, the Scottish Tourist Board (erstwhile) has previously shown its sensitivity while promoting Scotland to the English market. McCrone *et al.* (1995: 82) have noted that the Scottish Tourist Board differentiated its promotional brochures to the overseas market and to the English market, keeping in view some of the traditional icons that might create uneasiness among the English audience: to the English market 'tartanry' and rampant rhetoric were rather subdued. However, choosing icons like Burns, or more radically Bruce, to mark Homecoming celebrations and at a time when nationalist sentiment in Scotland is at its strongest, shows such events are not exclusively informed by professional considerations alone.

Sim and Leith (2013) argue that following devolution, the focus of diaspora tourism in Scotland has become more 'national' and that this has moved Scotland and its diaspora closer together. They also note that the creation of the Scottish Affairs Office in Washington, DC has helped develop closer cultural and business links with the Scottish diaspora in the United States: and they view these developments as reflecting an overall strategy operating across all political parties since devolution. However, Homecoming Scotland 2009 was not free of allegations of being hijacked politically by the Scottish Nationalist Party in government. According to Fairweather (2009), nationalist politics was omnipresent in Homecoming 2009 by the conspicuous presence of Scotland's First Minister Alex Salmond throughout the year. Salmond is the biggest nationalist mascot in Scotland. Fairweather also opined the use of Sir Sean Connery for the electronic advertisement for Homecoming Scotland as a political act. He appeared in the Homecoming Scotland 2009 advertisement declaring his love for Scotland, reciting a verse from Dougie MacLean's song 'Caledonia': 'Let me tell you that I love you and I think about you all the time.' Sir Sean Connery is also the Scottish Nationalist Party's poster boy and has supported a devolved parliament on earlier occasions by intoning stirring lines quoting the Declaration of Arbroath: 'It is not for glory. It is not for riches. Neither is it for honour. But it is for liberty that we fight and contend – which no honest man will lose but on his life' (Ross, 2000: 97–98). He is the biggest international icon who openly supports the nationalists in their demand for full Scottish independence and their choice of him in the Homecoming 2009 advertisement is highly significant.

Conclusions

We have seen in this chapter that the strong association between ancestral travel and its positive relation to an enhanced root identity also resonates with nationalism, because a strong sense of Scottishness, belonging to an authentic nation and a desire for an independent Scotland are linked with the ideals of nationalists. Travel to a homeland by a diaspora community has an immense effect in enriching and reinforcing 'root' identity. A close relationship between ethnicity and roots in the study of nations and nationalism makes the yearnings for roots and an ethnic past importantly tied to the idea of nativeness. In this context, celebrating Scottish icons in the name of tourism promotion to diasporic communities is meaningful.

Many travellers are of the opinion that their ancestral trip has a lasting impact, both on their understanding of their origins and on their identity in the present, and can bring forth a desire for return. This desire for return is manifested through repeat visits and their 'return' is thus a journey to a landscape of memory, one that is reached through the work of the imagination (Louie, 2001: 352). Strong identification with a distant homeland results in a degree of separation from the host society and often manifests itself in an 'in extremis' form of cultural life more intensively national than that currently evident in the homeland (Leonard, 2005; cf. Hughes & Allen, 2010). This was shown in this chapter: some respondents felt that life in Scotland was less Scottish than that back home in their adopted land.

However, there arises a pertinent question: where does this authority of tourism as a nationalistic force come from? The answer can be found in the fact that tourism has a vast organic role in the making of peoples, in the manufacture of places and in the manipulation of pasts (Hollinshead, 1998). This organic role of tourism in manipulating people, place and past can be an immense repository in the forming of an organic identity. Smith (1991: 9) makes the point that the awareness of an organic identity is importantly related to the idea of nation:

> A historic land is one where terrain and people have exerted mutual, and beneficial, influence over several generations. The homeland becomes a repository of historic memories and associations, the place where 'our' sages, saints and heroes lived, worked, prayed and fought. All this makes the homeland unique. Its rivers, coasts, lakes, mountains and cities become 'sacred' – places of veneration and exaltation whose inner meanings can be fathomed by the initiated, that is, the self-aware members of the nation.

In this chapter we have seen the way diasporas' visits to their native lands connect with the notion of 'homeland' nationalism. The importance of diasporas comes from the fact that the 'true nation' is imagined as a 'moral community' being formed centrally by the 'natives' in exile (Malkki, 1992). Travel to one's roots and heritage gives a sense of belongingness and reconnection with their root identity and realises their authentic self. This realisation has the propensity to reinforce one's cultural identity and helps create solidarity with their ancestral homeland and its people. This happens because of common ancestry. This solidarity is directed towards nationalism, because nationalism can strongly be associated with 'a consciousness of belonging to the nation, its sentiments and aspirations' (Smith, 1991: 72). Amidst such a backdrop, celebrations and events like 'Homecoming', aimed at attracting genealogical tourists, can be meaningfully nationalistic.

At the personal level, to the genealogical tourists with Scottish ancestry, touring Scotland is a means to reflect on their identity and on their sense of self and cultural roots. To the visitors with Scottish ancestral roots, a visit to Scotland is one of the ways through which they express their 'national' feelings and love for their native soil. Their travel is more than an ordinary holiday: it is a journey to their homeland and builds emotional bonding with the ancient nationhood. This chapter showed us that the ethnic element, which is a part of Scotland's 'national' community, is not confined within its national boundary. The narratives of Scotland also originate from beyond its national border, in the sentiments and expressions of emigrant communities living abroad. For these hyphenated communities, visiting Scotland is a way to connect and communicate emotionally with their native home and articulate their 'homeland' nationalism.

8 Conclusions

I started this book with a quest to ascertain if tourism in Scotland is an expression of nationalism. Some of the symbols and markers of Scottish culture in tourism examined in this book have shown us how they create and assert a collective or a distinctive identification of Scotland. The touristic heritage of Scotland also appears to persistently represent its cultural identity, 'national' image and characteristics in various forms and ways. This study leads us to view tourism as a narrative, in which nation, nationhood and national identity are recurring themes that are expressed in various forms and through a variety of means. For instance, this was revealed in the form of the oral narrative of tour guides; the obtrusive narrative in the form of museum displays and heritage preservation; the semiotics of image and icons and the personal accounts of genealogical tourists. All of these narratives assemble the iconography of the Scottish nation and culture and construct the 'national' imagery of Scotland.

The nature of narrative is varied. It is both forward and backward in direction, and creates a dialogue: (i) between the Scottish past and present; to an extent (ii) between the cultural and political domains of Scotland, and (iii) between 'native' Scotland and its emigrant communities. All of these dialogues are interlinked. There are many ways that tourism represents the Scottish past to visitors. In this book we looked at this through the verbal narratives of the guides; the developing touristic heritage of heroic figures, importing a more identifiable heritage for tourists; through the notion of the authenticity of cultural heritage; and by employing roots identity to reach genealogical visitors. These efforts not only inform visitors about particular sites or attractions but they educate and interpret the Scottish past.

In doing so, they make a statement of Scottish culture that has a strong resonance with nationalism and politics, though some of them may be more direct than others. For instance, the tour guides on the Edinburgh bus tour were assembling the various ingredients of the Scottish nation and making a constant reference to its relevance in contemporary Scotland. In lieu of the fact that a national capital city is a 'source of national imagery' (Maitland & Ritchie,

2009: 14), Edinburgh, through the guides' narratives, performs the symbolic function of 'representing the image and identity of the nation' (Huang & Santos, 2011: 23). Through Edinburgh's heritage, tour guides articulate Scottish national identity when they mention the devolution of the Scottish Parliament, Scottish military might, or Scotland's national existence. A similar case was visible with the trustees of the Robert the Bruce Commemoration Trust, some of whom believe that the heritage of Robert the Bruce has a political significance for the south-west region. Even in the case of Robert Burns and the 'Homecoming' celebrations, we observe a tenuous link that suggests Scottish culture is being mobilised for political gains by the Scottish Nationalist Party government.

The language of the dialogue created by tourism narratives is not equivocal, but it varies depending upon the nature of heritage icons and images, their historical significance, iconic stature, visitor perception and the ideology such objects represent to visitors. For example, the Edinburgh guides are more explicit and vocal in asserting the political aspect of Scottish nationhood while introducing the Scottish Parliament and making a distinction with England, but less vocal on other landmarks. Similarly, regional heritage in the south-west region is reasonably voluble in maintaining the cultural distinctiveness of Scotland. Some icons are direct and forcefully 'nationalistic' like Robert the Bruce where others are tacit or reticently 'nationalist', for example, Robert Burns. These various examples show that tourism is an outlet to assert and affirm a sense of the Scottish nation to visitors.

This book also shows the political side of tourism that is associated with the recreation and touristification of cultural heritage. The case of Robert the Bruce shows that though he is strongly associated with the south-west region his heritage largely remained neglected and unexploited commercially until recently. The success of Stirling in attracting tourists largely because of the appeal of Bruce's heritage has inspired Bruce enthusiasts in the south-west region who are also informed by the kind of 'nationalistic' vibe his appeal can create in the Scottish government and with the Nationalists in parliament. Their effort to develop his heritage for tourists is relatively new and in this sense Bruce's heritage is a recreated one for the region. This instance of recreation coalesces into nationalistic ideology by producing a uniform generic culture and encouraging the dominant version of history. It is helping nationalists by silencing the competing claims within Scotland regarding Scottish national identity and asserting a more popular historic past.

Scotland is a heritage-driven and identity-seeking nation (King, 2007). Tourism is so overwhelmed with images and icons, which are symbols of its cultural identity, that in many ways they become a statement of its identity. It has a topical significance as the 'descriptions of a specific culture are necessarily static snapshots at a given moment' (Burns & Novelli, 2006: 4). The strong assertion of Scottish cultural identity in the touristic heritage of Scotland in the current political scenario means that tourism is also a collaborator in the Nationalist project. An important characteristic of the Nationalists is that they are skillful operators of symbols and icons. For Scottish Nationalists, the mobilisation of Bannockburn or the image of Robert the Bruce and Robert Burns in tourism can be meaningful politically. The announcement by Scotland's First Minister Alex Salmond to hold the referendum for independence in 2014 is of great relevance here because the year 2014 marks the 700th anniversary of the battle of Bannockburn and it also coincides with the second Homecoming celebrations: planned within less than five years of the first celebration in 2009. The Nationalists' love for Homecoming in Scotland is not only as a result of the economic and cultural significance it brings to Scotland, but it is strongly tied to its ability to bolster nationalist feeling that can be politically meaningful for them and the planned referendum. This also suggests that the role of tourism as a narrative of a nation can be politically significant. In this instance, nationalism intersects with Nationalism because the 'national' icons in Scottish tourism representations are identifiers of Scottish nation and nationhood, and effectively articulate the idea of Scottish nation – resonating closely with the ideals of Nationalists.

Importantly, this work reasserts the idea that tourism and nationalism are interrelated concepts. Both are strongly grounded in the separation between 'us' and 'them', from which we draw a sense of 'who we are', which is an important way in which we make 'comparisons with those not in our group, but who belong to other groups' (Burns & Novelli, 2006: 1). Conforming to what Burns and Novelli (2006) outline, tourism's supply side in Scotland includes localised culture and people that showcase its national distinctiveness. It also presents a collective or a 'national' narrative of Scotland, in which the Scottish nation, nationhood and national identity are a recurring theme and is expressed in various forms and through a variety of means. This fact adds to the idea I put forward at the beginning of this book that Scotland is a 'touristified' nation, with its nationness highly exposed and exploited by tourism, mobilising some of the most potent markers of Scottish identity and culture.

The case of Scotland adds to the existing body of knowledge on the interface between tourism, nations and nationalism. There have been very few attempts to see the existence of nation, nationalism and national identity in tourism, while some scholars have suggested that some sites are specifically oriented towards representing collective identities (Franklin, 2003; Frew & White, 2011; Park, 2010, 2011; Pitchford, 2006; Pretes, 2003).

However, we have also seen that all tourism sites have elements that produce and reiterate the 'nation' and 'nationhood' in their narrative, albeit in different ways and senses; and that it may not be uniform, salient or equally distributed across all sites. This is consistent with Frew and White (2011), who argue that tourism overlaps, intersects with and traverses national identity. But I differ from Frew and White in my opinion of the implications of such relations. They argue for the development of national identity-related products, whereas this study cautions that tourism products can be heavily loaded with political and ideological connotations. It is mainly the role of agencies to decide what side of it to represent and interpret to visitors. Deliberately choosing or developing a national identity-related product raises the question of whether such a product is appropriate or not, particularly in Scotland where this could be counterproductive because of the large number of English visitors.

By manifesting 'national' or cultural identity, tourism authenticates the existence of the nation; assigning something as authentic is a subjective judgement and is a perception rather than a presentation of actual artefacts. This role of tourism has an ideological side. Many regimes, mainly repressive ones, have used tourism politically as a tool to make an ideological statement, an area that has started to attract scholars' attention (C.M. Hall, 1994; D. Hall, 1999; D.R. Hall, 1998; Kim *et al.*, 2007; Leong, 1989; Light, 2001). But unlike in earlier cases, I do not suggest that authorities necessarily have to make this their policy. In Scotland there is no strong evidence to suggest that public policy is driven by this objective. Instead, with reference to Scotland, this study makes a note that 'nation' and national identity are inherently present in Scottish tourism: the reason for this could be attributed to its particular heritage attractions.

This association between tourism and 'nation' or 'nationalism' presented in this book is important in the study of nationalism, which has notably disregarded the discourse of nationalism produced in alternative media like tourism. Looking from the economic perspective, Bond *et al.* (2003) argue that, informed by the past, economic agents mobilise national identity through the process of reiteration, recapture, reinterpretation and repudiation. The finding in this book also reinforces this idea, as tourism is one of the economic agents of a country. It shows that by becoming a communication between the past and present in Scotland, tourism mediates the Scottish nation, and advances its national sense through re-creation, authentication or touristification of its cultural heritage. Additionally, it opens a debate on the role of tourism in the expression of 'homeland' nationalism, an area that has been completely overlooked by scholars. Diasporas and other transnational acts can play a role in the development of a kind of nationalism, which is directed outward, across the boundaries of territory and directed towards members of their own ethnic nationality (Anderson, 1992; Brubaker, 1996; Mulligan, 2002; Schiller & Fouron, 2002). In this form, nationalism brings together those who share a sense of 'peoplehood' based on shared culture and history by situating people in their ancestral homeland. For people of Scottish descent, Scotland is strongly bound to their personal identity. Travelling to Scotland becomes a journey that instils a renewed sense of self-identity, enhances cultural affinity to their 'homeland' nation, and plays a role in articulating 'homeland' nationalism.

The observations made in this book can be helpful in understanding, identifying and bridging the gap between touristic image and the social reality of a nation. They also help us gain a deeper insight into the coherency between cultural and political spheres in touristic representations. In Scotland, this knowledge could be helpful to regional tourism agencies in devising tourism plans for their region. It can make them aware that projecting popular imagery can be an easy option in terms of gaining a promotional edge because of its easy identification, but it could also pose a threat to the region's distinctiveness and may lead to a weakening of its authentic identity. To the south-west region, a strong regional identity can give a substantial boost towards creating a distinctive touristic imagery of this region to visitors. To the Scottish diaspora communities, tourism can be a medium to connect with their 'native' land and reinforce their sense of affinity with the Scottish nation.

This book provides us with some of the evidence to support the view that there is an ideological confluence between tourism and nationalism. Through a variety of means motivated by history, heritage, a sense of identity and cultural roots, and authenticity, tourism converges with the idea of nationalism. The relationship is mutual and political in the sense that the existence of a 'nation' is a strong way to separate 'us' from 'them', and tourism is a medium to express this distinctiveness. Despite the lopsided imagery of Scotland in tourism, the evidence presented in this book indicates that there is a vibrant form of 'nationalism' in the touristic heritage of Scotland and it transcends political boundaries. Importantly, it offers an alternative method through which the Scottish nation is imagined and nationalism is expressed continually in Scotland, which is happening every day at various tourist sites, heritage attractions and through various cultural icons. Tourists consume the cultural component of a society, but there is an inextricable link between culture and identity – within which lie the ideas of 'nation', 'nationhood' and 'nationalism'.

References

Aitchison, C. (1999) Heritage and nationalism: Gender and the performance of power. In D. Crouch (ed.) *Leisure/Tourism Geographies* (pp. 59–73). London: Routledge.

Aitchson, P. and Cassell, A. (2003) *The Lowland Clearances: Scotland's Silent Revolution 1760–1830*. East Linton: Tuckwell.

Alderson, W. and Low, S. (1985) *Interpretation of Historic Sites*. Nashville, TN: American Association for State and Local History.

Ancestral Scotland (2010) See www.ancestralscotland.com (accessed 16 March 2010).

Anderson, B. (1991) *Imagined Communities: Reflections on the Origin and Spread of Nationalism*. London: Verso.

Anderson, B. (1992) *Long-Distance Nationalism: World Capitalism and the Rise of Identity Politics*. Amsterdam: Centre for Asian Studies Amsterdam.

Ap, J. and Wong, K.K.S. (2001) Case study on tour guiding: Professionalism, issues and problems. *Tourism Management* 22 (2), 551–563.

Ascherson, N. (2010) Liquidator. Book review of *Hugh Trevor-Roper: The Biography* by Adam Sisman. *London Review of Books*. See http://www.lrb.co.uk/v32/n16/neal-ascherson/liquidator (accessed 22 January 2012).

Ashworth, G. (1994) From history to heritage product: From heritage to identity. In G.J. Ashworth and P.J Larkham (eds) *Building New Heritage* (pp. 13–30). London: Routledge.

Ashworth, G.J. (1991) *Heritage Planning: Conservation as the Management of Urban Change*. Groningen: Geopers.

Atkinson, P. and Hammersley, M. (1994) Ethnography and participant observation. In N.K. Denzin and Y.S. Lincoln (eds) *Handbook of Qualitative Research* (pp. 248–261). Thousand Oaks, CA: Sage.

Baedeker, K. (1900) *Paris and Environs* (14th rev. edn). Leipzig: Karl Baedeker.

Bardsley, A. (2002) In and around the borders of the nation in Scott's *Guy Mannering*. *Nineteenth-Century Contexts* 24 (4), 397–415.

Barrow, G.W.S. (1988) *Robert Bruce and the Community of the Realm of Scotland*. Edinburgh: Edinburgh University Press.

Barth, F. (1981) Ethnic groups and boundaries. In *Process and Form in Social Life: Selected Essays of Fredrik Barth: Volume 1* (pp. 198–227). London: Routledge & Kegan Paul.

Barthes, R. (1977) The death of the author. In *Roland Barthes: Image Music Text: Essays Selected and Translated by Stephen Heath* (pp. 142–148). London: Fontana Press.

Basu, P. (2004) My own island home: The Orkney homecoming. *Journal of Material Culture* 9 (1), 27–42.

Basu, P. (2007) *Highland Homecomings: Genealogy and Heritage Tourism in the Scottish Diaspora*. London: Routledge.

Bechhofer, F. and McCrone, D. (2009) *National Identity, Nationalism and Constitutional Change*. Basingstoke: Palgrave MacMillan.

Begg, H.M. and Stewart, J.A. (1971) The nationalist movement in Scotland. *Journal of Contemporary History* 6 (1), 135–152.

Berghoff, H. and Korte, B. (2002) Britain and the making of modern tourism an interdisciplinary approach. In H. Berghoff, B. Korte, R. Schneider and C. Harvie (eds) *The Making of Modern Tourism* (pp. 1–20). New York: Palgrave.

Bhabha, H. (1990) *Nations and Narration*. London: Routledge.

Bhandari, K. (2008) Touristification of cultural resources: A case study of Robert Burns. *TOURISM: An International Interdisciplinary Journal* 56 (3), 283–293.

Bhandari, K. (2010a) Burnishing nationalism: Touring Burns and authenticity in Scotland. *Tourism Culture and Communication* 10 (2), 137–147.

Bhandari, K. (2010b) Tourism in Nepal: Post-monarchy challenges. *Journal of Tourism and Cultural Change* 8 (1), 69–83.

Bhandari, K. (2011) Recreating heritage in the southwest of Scotland. *Current Issues in Tourism* 14 (7), 669–683.

Bhandari, K. (2013) Imagining the Scottish nation: Tourism and homeland nationalism in Scotland. *Current Issues in Tourism*. DOI: 10.1080/13683500.2013.789005.

Bianchini, F. and Schwengel, H. (2001) Re-imaging the city. In J. Corner and S. Harvey (eds) *Enterprise and Heritage Crosscurrents of National Culture* (pp. 207–228). London: Routledge.

Billig, M. (1995) *Banal Nationalism*. London: Sage.

Billig, M. (2001) *Banal Nationalism*. London: Sage.

Blom, T. (2000) Morbid tourism – A postmodern market niche with an example of Althorp. *Norwegian Journal of Geography* 54 (1), 29–36.

Bold, A. (1991) *A Burns Companion*. Basingstoke: Macmillan.

Bond, R., McCrone, D. and Brown, A. (2003) National identity, and economic development: Reiteration, recapture, reinterpretation and repudiation. *Nations and Nationalism* 9 (3), 371–391.

Bond, R. and Rosie, M. (2002) National identities in post-devolution Scotland. *Scottish Affairs* 40, 34–53.

Bowman, G. (1992) The politics of tour guiding: Israeli and Palestinian guides in Israel and the Occupied Territories. In D. Harrison (ed.) *Tourism and Less Developed Countries* (pp. 121–134). London: Belhaven.

Brand, J., Mitchell, J. and Surridge, P. (1994) Social constituency and ideological profile: Scottish nationalism in the 1990s. *Political Studies* XLII, 616–629.

Braziel, J.E. and Mannur, A. (2003) Nation, migration, globalisation: Points of contention in diaspora studies. In J.E. Braziel and A. Mannur (eds) *Theorising Diaspora* (pp. 1–22). Oxford: Blackwell.

Brennan, T. (1990) The national longing for form. In H. Bhabha (ed.) *Nation and Narration* (pp. 44–70). London: Routledge.

Brock, J.M. (1999) *The Mobile Scot: A Study of Emigration and Migration 1861–1911*. Edinburgh: John Donald Publishers Ltd.

Brubaker, R. (1996) *Nationalism Reframed: Nationhood and the National Question in the New Europe*. Cambridge: Cambridge University Press.

Burns, P. and Novelli, M. (2006) Tourism and social identities: Introduction. In P. Burns and M. Novelli (eds) *Tourism and Social Identities: Global Frameworks and Local Realities* (pp. 1–11). Oxford: Elsevier Butterworth-Heinemann.

Burns, P.M. (2004) Social identities, globalisation and cultural politics of tourism. In W. Theobald (ed.) *Global Tourism* (pp. 391–405). Oxford: Butterworth-Heinemann.

Burrell, S.A. (1964) The apocalyptic vision of the early Covenanters. *The Scottish Historical Review* 43 (135), 1–24.
Butler, R.W. (1985) Evolution of tourism in the Scottish Highlands. *Annals of Tourism Research* 12 (3), 371–391.
Butler, R.W. (1998) Tartan mythology, the traditional tourist image of Scotland. In R. Ringer (ed.) *Destinations: Cultural Landscape of Tourism* (pp. 121–139). London: Routledge.
Carnegie, E. and McCabe, S. (2008) Re-enactment events and tourism: Meaning, authenticity and identity. *Current Issues in Tourism* 11 (4), 349–368.
Carrell, S. (2012) Scottish independence referendum: Why autumn 2014? See www.guardian.co.uk/politics/2012/jan/11/scottish-independence-referendum-autumn-2014 (accessed 12 February 2012).
Carter, S. (2004) Mobilising hrvatsko: Tourism and politics in the Croatian diaspora. In T. Coles and D.J. Timothy (eds) *Tourism Diasporas and Space* (pp. 188–201). London: Routledge.
Cheape, H. (1995) *Tartan: The Highland Habit*. Edinburgh: National Museums of Scotland.
Cheung, S.C.H. (1999) The meaning of a heritage trail in Hong Kong. *Annals of Tourism Research* 26 (3), 570–588.
Chhabra, D. (2008) Positioning museums on an authenticity continuum. *Annals of Tourism Research* 35 (2), 427–447.
Chhabra, D., Healy, R. and Sills, E. (2003) Staged authenticity and heritage tourism. *Annals of Tourism Research* 30 (3), 702–719.
City of Edinburgh Council (2009) See www.edinburgh.gov.uk (accessed 12 November 2009).
Cohen, A.P. (1985a) *The Symbolic Construction of Community*. London: Routledge.
Cohen, E. (1985b) The tourist guide: The origins, structure and dynamics of role. *Annals of Tourism Research* 12 (1), 456–477.
Cohen, A.P. (1996) Personal nationalism: A Scottish view of some rites, rights, and wrongs. *American Ethnologist* 23 (4), 802–815.
Cohen, C.B. (2010) *Take Me to My Paradise: Tourism and Nationalism in the British Virgin Islands*. London: Rutgers University Press.
Cohen, E. (1988) Authenticity and commoditization of tourism. *Annals of Tourism Research* 15 (3), 371–386.
Cohen, E. (1979) A phenomenology of tourist types. *Sociology* 13 (2), 179–201.
Cohen, E. (1993) The study of touristic images of native people: Mitigating the stereotype of a stereotype. In D.G. Pearce and R.W. Butler (eds) *Tourism Research: Critiques and Challenges* (pp. 36–69). London: Routledge.
Cohen, E. (2004) *Contemporary Tourism: Diversity and Change*. London: Elsevier.
Cole, S. (2007) Beyond commodification and authenticity. *Annals of Tourism Research* 34 (4), 943–960.
Coles, T. and Timothy, D.J. (2004a) 'My field is the world': Conceptualising diasporas, travel and tourism. In T. Coles and D.J. Timothy (eds) *Tourism Diasporas and Space* (pp. 1–29). London: Routledge.
Coles, T. and Timothy, D.J. (2004b) *Tourism, Diasporas and Space*. London: Routledge.
Connor, W. (2001) Homelands in a world of states. In M. Guibernau and J. Huchison (eds) *Understanding Nationalism* (pp. 53–73). Cambridge: Polity Press.
Cook, T. (1861) *Cook's Scottish Tourist Official Directory*. Leicester: T. Cook.

Cosgrove, D. (1994) Terrains of power. *Times Higher Education Supplement*, 11 March.
Cowan, E.J. (2002) The Covenanting tradition in Scottish history. In E.J. Cowan and R. Finlay (eds) *Scottish History: The Power of the Past* (pp. 121–146). Edinburgh: Edinburgh University Press.
Cowan, E.J. (2003) *'For Freedom Alone': The Declaration of Arbroath, 1320*. East Linton: Tuckwell Press.
Cowan, E.J. (2007) *The Wallace Book*. Edinburgh: John Donald Publishers Ltd.
Cowan, E.J. and Gifford, D. (1999) Introduction. In E.L Cowan and D. Gifford (eds) *The Polar Twins* (pp. 1–18). Edinburgh: John Donald Publishers Ltd.
Cowan, I.B. (1968) The Covenanters: A revision article. *The Scottish Historical Review* 47 (143), 35–52.
Craig, B. (1989) Interpreting the historic scene: The power of imagination in creating a sense of historic place. In D.L. Uzzell (ed.) *Heritage Interpretation, Volume 1: The Natural and Built Environment* (pp. 107–112). London: Belhaven,
Crang, M. (1996) Magic kingdom or quixotic quest for authenticity. *Annals of Tourism Research* 23 (2), 415–431.
Crespi-Vallbona, M. and Richards, G. (2007) The meaning of cultural festivals. *International Journal of Cultural Policy* 13 (1), 103–122.
Culler, J. (1988) *Framing the Sign: Criticism and its Institutions*. Oxford: Basil Blackwell.
Cuthill, V. (2004) Little England's global conference centre: Harrogate. In M. Sheller and J. Urry (eds) *Tourism Mobilities* (pp. 55–66). London: Routledge.
Dahles, H. (1996) The social construction of Mokum: Tourism and the quest for local identity in Amsterdam. In J. Boissevain (ed.) *Coping with Tourists* (pp. 227–246). London: Routledge.
Dahles, H. (2002) The politics of tour guiding. *Annals of Tourism Research* 29 (3), 783–800.
Davidson, N. (2000) *The Origins of Scottish Nationhood*. London: Pluto Press.
De Bres, K. and Davis, J. (2001) Celebrating group and place identity: A case study of a new regional festival. *Tourism Geographies* 3 (3), 326–337.
Defoe, D. (1971) *A Tour Through the Whole Island of Great Britain*. London: Penguin Books (originally published 1724–1726).
Del Casino, Jr. V. and Hanna, S.P. (2000) Representations and identities in tourism map spaces. *Progress in Human Geography* 24 (1), 23–46.
Denzin, N.K. and Lincoln, Y.S. (2005) *The Sage Handbook of Qualitative Research*. Thousand Oaks, CA: Sage.
Devine, T.M. (1994) *Clanship to Crofters' War: The Social Transformation of the Scottish Highlands*. Manchester: Manchester University Press.
Devine, T.M. (1999) A conservative people? Scottish gaeldom in the age of improvement. In T.M. Devine and J.R. Young (eds) *Eighteenth Century Scotland New Perspective* (pp. 225–236). East Linton: Tuckwell Press.
Devine, T.M. (2000) *The Scottish Nation*. London: Penguin.
Dewar, K. (1989) Interpretation as attraction. *Recreation Research Review* 14 (4), 45–49.
Dochery, T. (2004) The existence of Scotland. In E. Bell and G. Miller (eds) *Scotland in Theory* (pp. 231–248). Amsterdam: Rodopi.
Donaldson, G. (1966) *The Scots Overseas*. London: Robert Hale.
Drabble, M. (1979) *A Writer's Britain: Landscape in Literature*. London: Thames and Hudson.
Dumfries and Galloway Regional Tourism Strategy 2011–2016 (undated) See www.dumgal.gov.uk/CHttpHandler.ashx?id = 6686&p= (accessed 20 November 2011).

Duncan A.A.M. (1966) The community of the realm of Scotland and Robert Bruce: A review. *The Scottish Historically Review* 45 (140), 184–201.

Duncan, A.A.M. (1992) War of the Scots, 1306–23. *Transactions of the Royal Historical Society* 6th series (ii), 125–151.

Durie, A. (1992) Tourism in Victorian Scotland: The case of Abbotsford. *Scottish Economic and Social History* 12, 42–54.

Durie, A.J. (2003) *Scotland for the Holidays, Tourism in Scotland c1780–1939*. Scotland: Tuckwell Press.

Durie, A. (2012) *Travels in Scotland 1788–1881: A Selection from Contemporary Tourist Journals*. Woodbridge: Scottish History Society & The Boydell Press.

Durie, A.J., Bradley, J. and Dupree, M. (2006) *Water is Best: The Hydros and Health Tourism in Scotland 1840–1940*. Edinburgh: John Donald.

Durie, A., Yeoman, I. and McMahon-Beattie, U. (2006) How the history of Scotland creates a sense of place. *Place Branding* 2 (1), 43–52.

Duval, D.T. (2002) The return-visit-return migration connection. In C.M. Hall and A. Williams (eds) *Tourism and Migration: New Relationships between Production and Consumption* (pp. 257–266). Dordrecht: Kluwer.

Duval, D.T. (2004) Conceptualising return visits: A transnational perspective. In T. Coles and D.J. Timothy (eds) *Tourism Diasporas and Space* (pp. 50–61). London: Routledge.

Edensor, T. (1997a) National identity and the politics of memory: Remembering Bruce and Wallace in symbolic space. *Environment and Planning D* 15 (2), 175–194.

Edensor, T. (1997b) Reading Braveheart: Representing and contesting Scottish identity. *Scottish Affairs* 21. See www.scottishaffairs.org/backiss/pdfs/sa21/sa21_Edensor.pdf (accessed 5 November 2011).

Edensor, T. (1998) *Tourists at the Taj: Performance and Meaning at a Symbolic Site*. London: Routledge.

Edensor, T. (2004) Reconstituting the Taj Mahal. In M. Sheller and J. Urry (eds) *Tourism Mobilities* (pp. 103–116). London: Routledge.

Edensor, T. (2005) Mediating William Wallace: Audio-visual technology in tourism. In D. Crouch, R. Jackson and F. Thompson (eds) *The Media & the Tourist Imagination* (pp. 105–118). London: Routledge.

Ekos (2010) *Homecoming Scotland 2009. Economic Impact*. Glasgow: Ekos.

Eriksen, T. (2004) Place kinship and the case for non-ethnic nations. *Nations and Nationalism* 10 (1–2), 49–62.

ESRC (2005) Devolution briefings: Towards a multicultural nationalism? Anglophobia and Islamophobia in Scotland. See www.devolution.ac.uk/pdfdata/Briefing%20 24%20-%20Hussain-Miller.pdf (accessed 28 April 2009).

Fairweather, E. (2009) Homecoming Scotland 2009: The benefits and drawbacks of high profile government intervention in Scotland's year-long nationwide celebration. In ATHE (Association of Tourism in Higher Education), *Navigating Shifting Sands and Moving Mountains: New Paradigms for Tourism and Tourism Education*. Peak District, UK, 2–4 December.

Fawcett, C. and Cormack, P. (2001) Guarding authenticity at literary tourism sites. *Annals of Tourism Research* 28 (3), 686–704.

Ferguson, W. (1998) *The Identity of the Scottish Nation*. Edinburgh: Edinburgh University Press.

Finlay, R.J. (1997) The Burns cult and Scottish identity in the nineteenth and twentieth centuries. In K. Simpson (ed.) *Love & Liberty: Robert Burns a Bicentenary Celebration* (pp. 69–78). East Lothian: Tuckwell Press.

Finlay, R.J. (1998) Unionism and the dependency culture: Politics and state intervention in Scotland, 1918–1997. In C.M.M. Macdonald (ed.) *Unionist Scotland 1800–1997* (pp. 100–116). Edinburgh: John Donaldson.

Finlay, R.J. (1999) Keeping the covenant: Scottish national identity. In T.M. Devine and J.R. Young (eds) *Eighteenth Century Scotland. New Perspectives* (pp. 122–133). East Linton: Tuckwell Press.

Foley, M. and Lennon, J.J. (1996) JFK and dark tourism: A fascination with assassination. *International Journal of Heritage Studies* 2 (4), 198–211.

Foucault, M. (1980) *Textual Strategies: Perspectives in Post Structural Criticism*, edited with an introduction by J.V. Harari. London: Methuen.

Fowler, S. (2003) Ancestral tourism. *Insights* March, D31–D36.

Franklin, A. (2003) *Tourism: An Introduction.* London: Sage.

Frew, E. and White, L. (2011) *Tourism and National Identities: An International Perspective.* London: Routledge.

Future Foundation and VisitScotland (2005) *Our Ambitions for Scottish Tourism: A Journey to 2025.* Edinburgh: Future Foundation and VisitScotland.

Gamble, A. (2006) The constitutional revolution in the United Kingdom. *The Journal of Federalism* 36 (1), 19–35.

Geekie, J. and Levy, R. (1989) Devolution and the tartanisation of the Labour Party. *Parliamentary Affairs* 42 (3), 399–411.

Gellner, E. (1999) *Nations and Nationalism.* Oxford: Blackwell Publishers.

Gillespie, S.A. (2011) Agri-tourism characteristics and contributions to destination and livelihood sustainability: A case study from south-west Scotland. In D.V.L. Macleod and S.A. Gillespie (eds) *Sustainable Tourism in Rural Europe: Approaches to Development* (pp. 210–229). London: Routledge.

Gold, J.R. and Gold, M.M. (1995) *Imagining Scotland: Tradition, Representation and Promotion in Scottish Tourism since 1750.* Aldershot: Scolar Press.

Graham, B. (1996) The contested interpretation of heritage landscapes in Northern Ireland. *International Journal of Heritage Studies* 2 (1–2), 10–22.

Graham, B., Ashworth, G.J. and Tunbridge, J.E. (2000) *A Geography of Heritage: Power, Culture and Economy.* London: Arnold.

Grenier, C.H. (2005) *Tourism and Identity in Scotland, 1770–1914: Creating Caledonia.* Aldershot: Ashgate.

Grenier, K.H. (2006) 'Scottishness', 'Britishness', and Scottish tourism, 1770–1914. *History Compass* 4 (6), 1000–1023.

Groome, F.H. (1894) *Ordinance Gazeteer of Scotland.* London: Mackenzie.

Gruffudd, P. (1994) Selling the countryside: Representations of rural Britain. In J.R. Gold and S.V. Ward (eds) *Place Promotion: The Use of Publicity and Public Relations to Sell Towns and Regions* (pp. 247–263). Chichester: John Wiley.

Gurung, G., Simmons, D. and Devlin, P. (1996) The evolving role of tour guides: The Nepali experience. In R. Butler and T. Hinch (eds) *Tourism and Indigenous Peoples* (pp. 107–128). London: International Thomson Business Press.

Haesly, R. (2005) Identifying Scotland and Wales: Types of Scottish and Welsh national identities. *Nations and Nationalism* 11 (2), 243–263.

Hague, E. (2002) The Scottish diaspora: Tartan day and the appropriation of Scottish identities in the United States. In D.C. Harvey, R. Jones, N. McInroy and C. Milligan (eds) *Celtic Geographies Old Culture New Times* (pp. 139–156). Routledge: London.

Hall, C.M. (1994) *Tourism and Politics: Policy, Power and Place.* Chichester: Wiley.

Hall, C.M. (2002) Tourism in capital cities. *TOURISM: An International Interdisciplinary Journal* 50 (3), 235–248.
Hall, C.M. (2003) Politics and place: Analysis of power in tourism communities. In S. Singh, D.J. Timothy and R.K. Dowling (eds) *Tourism in Destination Communities* (pp. 99–113). Wallingford: CAB International.
Hall, C.M. (2004) Reflexivity and tourism research. In J. Phillimore and L. Goodson (eds) *Qualitative Research in Tourism: Ontologies, Epistemologies and Methodologies* (pp. 137–155). London: Routledge.
Hall, C.M. (2007) Response to Yeoman *et al.*: The fakery of 'The authentic tourist'. *Tourism Management* 28 (4), 1139–1140.
Hall, C.M. and McArthur, S. (1996) *Heritage Management in New Zealand and Australia: The Human Dimension.* Melbourne: Oxford University Press.
Hall, D. (1999) Destination branding, niche marketing and national image projection in central and eastern Europe. *Journal of Vacation Marketing* 5 (3), 227–237.
Hall, D. (2002) Branding and national identity: The case of central and eastern Europe. In N. Morgan, A. Pritchard and R. Pride (eds) *Destination Branding: Creating the Unique Destination Proposition* (pp. 87–105). Oxford: Butterworth-Heinemann.
Hall, D.R. (1998) Central and eastern Europe: Tourism, development and transformation. In A.M. Williams and G. Shaw (eds) *Tourism and Economic Development: European Experiences* (pp. 345–370). Chichester: Wiley.
Hall, S. (1996) Who needs identity? In S. Hall and P. Gay (eds) *Questions of Cultural Identity* (pp. 1–17). London: SAGE Publication.
Hanham, H.J. (1968) The Scottish nation faces the post-imperial world. *International Journal* 23 (2), 570–584.
Hart-Davis, D. (1978) *Monarchs of the Glen*. London: J. Cape.
Harvie, C. (1998) *Scotland and Nationalism*. Routledge: London.
Hasting, A. (1997) *The Construction of Nationhood*. Cambridge: Cambridge University Press.
Hay, B. (2007) Lessons for the future: The history and development of the Scottish Tourist Board. In V.T.C. Middleton (ed.) *British Tourism: The Remarkable Story of Growth* (pp. 151–158). London: Butterworth-Heinemann.
Hearn, J. (2000) *Claiming Scotland: National Identity and Liberal Culture*. Edinburgh: Polygon.
Hechter, M. (1975) *Internal Colonialism: The Celtic Fringe in British National Development, 1536–1966*. London: Routledge
Henderson, J. (2001) Heritage, identity and tourism in Hong Kong. *International Journal of Heritage Studies* 7 (3), 219–235.
Herbert, D. (2003) Literary places and tourism. In D.V.L. Macleod (ed.) *Niche Tourism in Question* (pp. 53–70). Dumfries: University of Glasgow Crichton Publications.
Hesse-Biber, S.N. and Leavy, P. (2006) *The Practice of Qualitative Research*. London: Sage Publications.
Hewison, R. (1987) *The Heritage Industry, Britain in a Climate of Decline*. London: Methuen London.
History Today (2010) Remembering Burns: The Robert Burns Birthplace Museum. See www.historytoday.com/blog/news-blog/kathryn-hadley/remembering-burns-robert-burns-birthplace-museum (accessed 27 October 2011).
Hobsbawm, E. (1983) Introduction: Inventing traditions. In E. Hobsbawm and T. Ranger (eds) *The Invention of Tradition* (pp. 1–14). Cambridge: Cambridge University Press.
Hobsbawm, E. (1999) *Nations and Nationalism since 1780*. Cambridge: Cambridge University Press.

Hodge, C.J. and Baranek, C.M. (2011) Dwelling: Transforming narratives at historic house museums. *International Journal of Heritage Studies* 17 (2), 97–101.
Holliday, A. (2007) *Doing and Writing Qualitative Research*. London: Sage Publications.
Hollinshead, K. (1998) Tourism and restless peoples: A dialectical inspection of Bhabha's halfway populations. *Tourism, Culture & Communication* 1 (1), 49–77.
Holloway, F.C. (1981) The guided tour: A sociological approach. *Annals of Tourism Research* 8 (3), 377–402.
Hooson, D. (1994) *Geography and National Identity*. Oxford: Blackwell.
Huang, W. and Santos, C. (2011) Tourism and national identity in the United States: The case of Washington, DC. In E. Frew and L. White (eds) *Tourism and National Identity: An International Perspective* (pp. 13–25). Abingdon: Routledge.
Hughes, G. (1992) Tourism and geographical imagination. *Leisure Studies* 11 (2), 31–42.
Hughes, G. (1995) Authenticity in tourism. *Annals of Tourism Research* 22 (4), 781–803.
Hughes, H. and Allen D. (2010) Holidays of the Irish diaspora: The pull of the 'homeland'? *Current Issues in Tourism* 13 (1), 1–19.
Hutchinson, J. (1999) Re-interpreting cultural nationalism. *Australian Journal of Politics and History* 45 (3), 392–407.
Ichijo, A. (2003) The uses of history: Anglo-British and Scottish views of Europe. *Regional and Federal Studies* 13 (3), 23–43.
Ichijo, A. (2004) *Scottish Nationalism and the Idea of Europe: Concepts of Europe and the Nation*. London: Routledge.
Inglis, D. and Holmes, M. (2003) Highlands and other haunts: Ghosts in Scottish tourism. *Annals of Tourism Research* 30 (1), 50–63.
Jacobson, R. (1960) Closing statement: Linguistics and poetics. In T.A. Sebeok (ed.) *Style in Language* (pp. 350–377). New York: John Willey and Sons.
Jamal, T. and Hill, S. (2004) Developing a framework for indicators of authenticity: The place and space of cultural and heritage tourism. *Asia Pacific Journal of Tourism Research* 9 (4), 353–371.
Johnson, S. and Boswell, J. (1984) *A Journey to the Western Islands of Scotland and The Journal of a Tour to the Hebrides*. London: Penguin Books.
Jorgensen, A. (2003) Power, knowledge and tour guiding: The construction of Irish identity on board country WickLow tour buses. In M. Cronin and B. O'Connor (eds) *Irish Tourism: Image, Culture and Identity* (pp. 141–157). Clevedon: Channel View Publications.
Kelly, M.E. (2000) Ethnic pilgrimages: Peoples of Lithuanian descent in Lithuania. *Sociological Spectrum* 20 (1), 65–91.
Kerr, W.R. and Wood, R.C. (1999) Scottish tourism after devolution? *Hospitality Review* April, 16–23.
Kim, S.S., Timothy, D.J. and Han, H. (2007) Tourism and political ideologies: A case of tourism in North Korea. *Tourism Management* 28 (4), 1031–1043.
King, B. (1980) *The New English Literatures*. London: Macmillan.
King, B. (1994) What is ethnic tourism? An Australian perspective. *Tourism Management* 15 (3), 173–176.
King, B. (2007) Response to Yeoman *et al.*: Competitive advantage through 'authenticity': An assessment of Scotland's tourism prospects. *Tourism Management* 28 (4), 1141–1143.
Kirshenblatt-Gimblett, B. (1998) *Destination Culture Tourism, Museums and Heritage*. London: University of California Press.
Koshar, R. (1998) 'What ought to be seen': Tourists' guidebooks and national identities in modern Germany and Europe. *Journal of Contemporary History* 33 (3), 323–340.

Kotler, P. and Gertner, D. (2002) Country as brand, product, and beyond: A place marketing and brand management perspective. *Journal of Brand Management* 9 (4–5), 249–261.
Lanfant, M.F. (1995a) Introduction. In M.F. Lanfant, J.B. Allcock and E.M. Bruner (eds) *International Tourism: Identity and Change* (pp. 1–23). London: Sage.
Lanfant, M.F. (1995b) International tourism, internationalization and challenge to identity. In M.F. Lanfant, J.B. Allcock and E.M. Bruner (eds) *International Tourism: Identity and Change* (pp. 24–43). London: Sage.
Lanfant, M.F., Allcock, J.B. and Bruner, E.M. (1995) *International Tourism: Identity and Change*. London: Sage.
Lannon, T. (1983) *The Making of Modern Stirling*. Stirling: Forth Naturalist and Historian.
Lee, G.W. (1976) North Sea oil and Scottish nationalism. *The Political Quarterly* 47 (3), 307–317.
Leite, N. (2005) Travels to an ancestral past: On diasporic tourism, embodied memory, and identity. *Antropologicas* 9, 273–302.
Leneman, L. (1987) The effects of Ossian on Lowland Scotland. In J.J. Carter and J.H. Pittock (eds) *Aberdeen and the Enlightenment* (pp. 357–362). Aberdeen: Aberdeen University Press.
Lennon, J. and Foley, M. (2000) *Dark Tourism: The Attraction of Death and Disaster*. London: Continuum.
Lennon, J.J. and Hay, B. (2003) *Benchmarking Scotland*. Edinburgh: VisitScotland.
Leonard, M. (2005) Performing identities: Music and dance in the Irish communities of Coventry and Liverpool. *Social and Cultural Geography* 6 (4), 515–529.
Leong, W.T. (1989) Culture and the state: Manufacturing traditions for tourism. *Critical Studies in Mass Communication* 6 (4), 355–375.
Lepp, A. and Haris, A. (2008) Tourism and national identity in Uganda. *International Journal of Tourism Research* 10 (6), 525–536.
Light, D. (2001) 'Facing the future': Tourism and Identity-building in post-socialist Romania. *Political Geography* 20 (8), 1053–1074.
Lindsay, M. (1994) *Robert Burns: The Man, His Work, The Legend*. London: Robert Hale.
Long, P. and Palmer, N. (2007) *Royal Tourism: Excursions around Monarchy*. Clevedon: Channel View Publications.
Louie, A. (2001) Crafting places through mobility: Chinese American 'roots searching' in China. *Identities* 8 (3), 343–379.
Lowenthal, D. (1975) Past time, present place: Landscape and memory. *Geographical Review* 65 (1), 1–36.
Lowanthal, D. (1985) *The Past is a Foreign Country*. Cambridge: Cambridge University Press.
Lowenthal, D. (1994) European and English landscapes as national symbols. In D. Hooson (ed.) *Geography and National Identity* (pp. 15–38). Oxford: Blackwell.
Lowenthal, D. (1998) *The Heritage Crusade and the Spoils of History*. Cambridge: Cambridge University Press.
Lowenthal, D. (2005) *The Past is a Foreign Country*. Cambridge: Cambridge University Press.
Lynch, M. (2005) *The Oxford Companion to Scottish History*. Oxford: Oxford University Press.
MacCannell, D. (1992) *Empty Meeting Grounds: The Tourist Papers*. London: Routledge.
MacCannell, D. (1999) *The Tourist: A New Theory of the Leisure Class*. Berkeley: University of California Press.
MacCormick, N. (2000) Is there a constitutional path to Scottish independence? *Parliamentary Affairs* 53, 721–736.

Macdonald, S. (1997) *Reimagining Culture: Histories, Identities and the Gaelic Renaissance.* London: Berg.
Macdonald, S. (2006) Mediating heritage: Tour guiding at the former Nazi Party rally grounds, Nuremberg. *Tourist Studies* 6 (2), 119–133.
MacGregor, N. (1991) Scholarship and the public. *Royal Society of Arts Journal* 139, 191–194.
MacLellan, R. (2010) Devolution – Towards independence: Tourism in Scotland in the 21st century. In R.W. Butler and W. Suntikul (eds) *Tourism and Political Change* (pp. 57–67). London: Goodfellow Publisher.
MacLellan, R. and Smith, R. (1998) *Tourism in Scotland.* London: International Thomson Business Press.
Macleod, D. (2009) Scottish theme towns: Have new identities enhanced development? *Journal of Tourism and Cultural Change* 7 (2), 133–145.
Macleod, D.V.L. (2010) Power, culture and the production of heritage. In D.V.L. Macleod and J.C. Carrier (eds) *Tourism, Power and Culture: Anthropological Insights* (pp. 64–89). Bristol: Channel View Publications.
Maitland, R. and Ritchie, B.W. (2009) City tourism: National capital perspectives. *City Tourism: National Capital Perspectives* (pp. 14–26). Oxfordshire: CAB International.
Malkki, L. (1992) National geographic: The rooting of peoples and the territorialisation of national identity among scholars and refugees. *Cultural Anthropology* 7 (1), 24–44.
McCain, G. and Ray, N.M. (2003) Legacy tourism: The search for personal meaning in heritage travel. *Tourism Management* 24 (6), 713–717.
McCrone, D. (1992) *Understanding Scotland: The Sociology of a Stateless Nation.* London: Routledge.
McCrone, D. (2001) *Understanding Scotland, the Sociology of a Nation* (2nd edn). London: Routledge.
McCrone, D. (2002) Tomorrow's ancestors: Nationalism, identity and history. In E.J. Cowan and R.J. Finlay (eds) *Scottish History: The Power of the Past* (pp. 253–271). Edinburgh: Edinburgh University of Press.
McCrone, D., Morris, A. and Kiely, R. (1995) *Scotland – The Brand: The Making of Scottish Heritage*. Edinburgh: Edinburgh University Press.
McCrone, D. and Paterson, L. (2002) The conundrum of Scottish independence. *Scottish Affairs* 40, 54–75.
McGuirk, C. (1994) Burns and nostalgia. In K. Simpson (ed.) *Burns Now* (pp. 31–69). Edinburgh: Canongate Academic.
McLean, F. (1998) Museums and the construction of national identity: A review. *International Journal of Heritage Studies* 3 (4), 244–252.
McLean, F. (2005) Guest editorial: Museums and national identity. *Museum and Society* 3 (1), 1–4.
McLean, F. and Cooke, S. (2003) Constructing the identity of a nation: The tourist gaze at the Museum of Scotland. *Tourism Culture and Communication* 4 (3), 153–162.
McManus, R. (2005) Identity crisis? Heritage construction, tourism and place marketing in Ireland. In M. McCarthy (ed.) *Ireland's Heritages: Critical Perspective on Memory and Identity* (pp. 235–250). Aldershot: Ashgate Publishing.
McNamee, C. (1997) *The Wars of the Bruces: Scotland, England and Ireland, 1306–1328.* East Linton: Tuckwell Press.
Meethan, K. (2001) *Tourism in Global Society, Place, Culture, Consumption*. Basingstoke: Palgrave.
Mellinger, W.M. (1994) Towards a critical analysis of tourism representations. *Annals of Tourism Research* 21 (4), 756–779.

Miles, S.T. (2012) Battlefield tourism: Meanings and interpretations. Unpublished PhD thesis, The University of Glasgow.
Mills, C.W. (1970) *The Sociological Imagination*. Harmondsworth: Penguin.
Mitchell, J. (1998) Contemporary unionism. In A.M.M. MacDonald (ed.) *Unionist Scotland 1800–1997* (pp. 117–139). Edinburgh: John Donald Publishers Ltd.
Mitchell, J. (2003) *Governing Scotland: The Invention of Administrative Devolution*. London: Palgrave.
Morgan, N. and Pritchard, A. (1998) *Tourism Promotion and Power: Creating Images, Creating Identities.* Chichester: John Wiley & Sons.
Morgan, N. and Pritchard, A. (2004) Mae'n Bryd I ddod Adref – *It's* time to come home: Exploring the contested emotional geographies of Wales. In C. Tim and D.J. Timothy (eds) *Tourism Diasporas and Space* (pp. 233–245). London: Routledge.
Morgan, N., Pritchard, A. and Pride, R. (2002) Marketing to the Welsh diaspora: The appeal to hiraeth and homecoming. *Journal of Vacation Marketing* 9 (1), 69–80.
Morton, G. (1993) Unionist-nationalism. The historical construction of Scottish national identity, Edinburgh 1830–1860. PhD thesis, University of Edinburgh.
Morton, G. (1999) *Unionist Nationalism. Governing Urban Scotland, 1830–1860.* East Linton: Tuckwell Press.
Mulligan, A.N. (2002) A forgotten 'greater Ireland': The transatlantic development of Irish nationalism. *Scottish Geographical Journal* 118 (3), 219–234.
Murdoch, A. (2010) *Scotland and America, c.1600–c.1800.* Basingstoke: Palgrave Macmillan.
Murdoch, J. (1852) *A Guide to the Highlands of Speyside*. Forres: C. Merrilees.
Nairn, T. (1981) *The Break-Up of Britain: Crisis and Neo-Nationalism.* London: Verso.
Nairn, T. (1995) Upper and lower cases. *London Review of Books*, 24 August, pp. 14–18.
Nairn, T. (1997) *Faces of Nationalism: Janus Revisited.* London: Verso.
Nash, C. (2002) Genealogical identities. *Environment and Planning D: Society and Space* 20 (1), 27–52.
Nettekoven, L. (1979) Mechanisms of intercultural interaction. In E. de Kadt (eds) *Tourism: Passport to Development?* (pp. 135–145). New York: Oxford University Press.
Neuman, W.L. (2003) *Social Research Methods: Qualitative and Quantitative Approaches.* London: Pearson Education.
Noble, A. (1994) Burns and Scottish nationalism. In K. Simpson (ed.) *Burns Now* (pp. 167–192). Edinburgh: Canongate Academic.
O'Dell, A.C. and Walton, K. (1962) *The Highlands and Islands of Scotland*. London: T. Nelson and Sons.
Olins, W. (2002) Branding the nation – The historical context. *Journal of Brand Management* 9 (4–5), 241–248.
Palmer, C. (1999) Tourism and the symbols of identity. *Tourism Management* 20 (3), 313–321.
Palmer, N.J. (2007) By royal association: British monarchy as a place representation tool. In P. Long and N.J. Palmer (eds) *Royal Tourism: Excursions around Monarchy* (pp. 159–180). Clevedon: Channel View Publications.
Park, H. (2010) Heritage tourism: Emotional journeys to nationhood. *Annals of Tourism Research* 37 (1), 116–135.
Park, H. (2011) Shared national memory as intangible heritage: Remaining two Koreans as one nation. *Annals of Tourism Research* 38 (2), 520–539.
Paterson, J.H. (1965) The novelist and his region: Scotland through the eyes of Sir Walter Scott. *Scottish Geographical Journal* 81 (3), 146–152.

Pennant, T. (1776) *A Tour in Scotland, 1769 and a Voyage to the Hebrides, 1772*. Dublin: A Leathley.

Pitchford, S. (2006) Identity tourism: A medium for Native American stories. *Tourism Culture and Communication* 6 (2), 85–105.

Pitchford, S. (2008) *Identity Tourism: Imaging and Imagining the Nation*. London: Elsevier.

Pitchford, S.R. (1995) Ethnic tourism and nationalism in Wales. *Annals of Tourism Research* 22 (1), 35–52.

Pittock, M. (2008) *The Road to Independence: Scotland since the Sixties*. London: Reaktion Books.

Pont, K.L. (1993) *Professional Guide: Dynamics of Tour Guiding*. New York: Van Nostrand Reinhold.

Prebble, J. (1982) *The Highland Clearances*. London: Penguin.

Pretes, M. (2003) Tourism and nationalism. *Annals of Tourism Research* 30 (1), 125–142.

Pritchard, A. and Morgan, N.J. (2001) Culture identity and tourism representation: Marketing Cymru or Wales? *Tourism Management* 22 (2), 167–179.

Pryde, G.S. (1935) The development of nationalism in Scotland. *The Sociological Review* 27 (3), 264–280.

Rayner, G. and Kirkup, J. (2008) Financial crisis: How the dream of Scottish independence died. *The Telegraph*. See www.telegraph.co.uk/finance/financialcrisis/3189935/Financial-crisis-How-the-dream-of-Scottish-independence-died.html (accessed 1 November 2011).

Reicher, S. and Hopkins, N. (2001) *Self and Nation: Categorization, Contestation and Mobilization*. London: Sage.

Reisinger, Y. and Steiner, C. (2006) Reconceptualising interpretation: The role of tour guides in authentic tourism. *Current Issues in Tourism* 9 (6), 481–498.

Renan, E. (1990) What is a nation? In H. Bhabha (ed.) *Nation and Narration* (pp. 8–22). London: Routledge.

Richter, L.K. (1999) The politics of heritage tourism development: Emerging issues for the new millennium. In D.G. Pearce and R. Butler (eds) *Contemporary Issues in Tourism Development* (pp. 108–126). London: Routledge.

Roche, M. (2000) *Mega-Events and Modernity*. London: Routledge.

Rojek, C. (1993) *Ways of Escape: Modern Transformations in Leisure and Travel*. London: Macmillan.

Rojek, C. and Urry, J. (1997) *Touring Cultures: Transformations of Travel and Theory*. London: Routledge.

Rose, G. (1995) Place and identity: A sense of place. In D. Massey and P. Jess (eds) *A Place in the World? Places, Culture and Globalisation* (pp. 87–132). New York: Oxford University Press.

Ross, A. (2000) Wallace's monument and the resumption of Scotland. *Social Text* 18 (4), 83–107.

Salazar, N.B. (2010) *Envisioning Eden: Mobilizing Imaginaries in Tourism and Beyond*. Oxford: Berghahn Books.

Santos, C.A. and Yan, G. (2010) Genealogical tourism a phenomenological examination. *Journal of Travel Research* 29 (1), 56–67.

Schiller, N.G. and Fouron, G. (2002) Long-distance nationalism defined. In J. Vincent (ed.) *The Anthropology of Politics* (pp. 356–365). Oxford: Blackwell Publishing.

Schimidt, C. (1979) The guided tour, insulated adventure, urban life. *A Journal of Ethnographic Research* 8, 441–468.

Schouten, F.F.J. (1995) Heritage as historical reality. In D.T. Herbert (ed.) *Heritage, Tourism and Society* (pp. 21–31). London: Pinter.

Scott, R.M. (1999) *Robert the Bruce: King of Scots*. Edinburgh: Canongate.

Scottish Executive (2006) *Scottish Tourism: The Next Decade – A Tourism Framework for Change*. Edinburgh: The Stationary Office.

Seaton, A.V. (1996) Guided by the dark: From thanatopsis to thanatourism. *International Journal of Heritage Studies* 2 (4), 234–244.

Selwyn, T. (1996) *The Tourist Image: Myth and Myth Making in Tourism*. Chichester: Wiley.

Shaffer, M.S. (2001) *See America First: Tourism and National Identity, 1880–1940*. Smithsonian Books.

Sharpley, R. and Stone, P. (2009) *The Darker Side of Travel: The Theory and Practice of Dark Tourism*. Bristol: Channel View Publications.

Sheffer, G. (1986) A new field of study: Modern diasporas in international politics. In G. Sheffer (ed.) *Modern Diasporas in International Politics* (pp. 1–15). London: Croom Helm.

Shulman, S. (2002) Challenging the civic/ethnic and west/east dichotomies in the study of nationalism. *Comparative Political Studies* 35 (5), 554–585.

Sim, D. and Leith, M. (2013) Diaspora tourists and the Scottish homecoming 2009. *Journal of Heritage Tourism*. DOI: 10.1080/1743873X.2012.758124.

Simpson, K. (1994) Introduction. In K. Simpson (ed.) *Burns Now* (pp. xi–xxv). Edinburgh: Canongate Academic.

Smith, A.D. (1991) *National Identity*. London: Penguin.

Smith, A.D. (1995) Gastronomy or geology? The role of nationalism in the reconstruction of nations. *Nations and Nationalism* 1 (1), 3–23.

Smith, A.D. (2008) *The Cultural Foundations of Nations*. Oxford: Blackwell Publishing.

Smith, L. (2006) *Uses of Heritage*. New York: Routledge.

Smith, M.K. and Forest, K. (2006) Enhancing vitality or compromising integrity? Festivals, tourism and the complexities of performing culture. In D. Picard and M. Robinson (eds) *Festivals, Tourism and Social Change* (pp. 133–151). Clevedon: Channel View Publications.

Smith, S.J. (1993) Bounding the borders: Claiming space and making place in rural Scotland. *Transactions of the Institute of British Geographers* 18 (3), 291–308.

Smith V.L. (1989) *Hosts and Guests: The Anthropology of Tourism*. Philadelphia: University of Pennsylvania Press.

Smout, T.C. (1994) Perspectives on the Scottish identity. *Scottish Affairs*. See www.scottishaffairs.org/backiss/pdfs/sa6/SA6_Smout.pdf (accessed 15 January 2011).

Squire, S.J. (1994) The cultural values of literary tourism. *Annals of Tourism Research* 21 (1), 103–120.

Squires, J.E. (undated) Intrinsic and extrinsic motivators in the Scottish nationalist movement. *Preliminary Draft of Paper for Presentation at the ISA Panel on Indigenous Peoples and Non-State Nations*. See www2.hawaii.edu/ ~ fredr/squires.htm (accessed 28 April 2009).

Stephenson, M.L. (2002) Travelling to the ancestral homelands: The aspirations and experiences of a UK Caribbean community. *Current Issues in Tourism* 5 (5), 378–425.

Stephenson, M.L. (2004) Tourism, racism and the UK Afro-Caribbean diaspora. In T. Coles and D.J. Timothy (eds) *Tourism Diasporas and Space* (pp. 62–77). London: Routledge.

Stevenson, D. (1988) *The Covenanters: The National Covenant and Scotland*. Stirling: The Saltire Society.

Stewart, D. (2004) Challenging the consensus: Scotland under Margaret Thatcher 1979–1990. PhD thesis, Glasgow University.

Stone, P. (2005) Consuming dark tourism: A call for research. *Review of Tourism Research* 3 (5), 109–117.

Swain, M. (2004) (Dis)embodied experience and power dynamics in tourism research. In J. Phillimore and L. Goodson (eds) *Qualitative Research in Tourism: Ontologies, Epistemologies and Methodologies* (pp. 102–118). London: Routledge.

The Border Gathering (2008) *The Border Gathering Leaflet.*

The Border Gathering (2009) The Border Gathering. See www.bordergathering.co.uk (accessed 20 October 2009).

The Bruce Trust (2009) *The Hero King Robert the Bruce*. See www.brucetrust.co.uk/home.html (accessed 20 December 2009).

The Galloway Project (1968) *A Study of the Economy of the South West of Scotland with Particular Reference to its Tourist Potential*. Edinburgh: Scottish Tourist Board.

The Globe Inn (2008) The Globe Inn. See www.globeinndumfries.co.uk/ (accessed 20 September 2009).

The Globe Inn (2011) See www.globeinndumfries.co.uk (accessed 12 December 2011).

The Morning Star (2007) SNP switch on Europe. See www.morningstaronline.co.uk/index.php/news/layout/set/print/content/view/full/51552 (accessed 1 November 2011).

The Scotsman (2008) Salmond targets Burns' Day for independence launch. See http://business.scotsman.com/scottishindependence/Salmond-targets-Burns39-Day-for.4080844.jp (accessed 1 March 2009).

The Scottish Government (2005) Robert Burns worth £160 million to Scottish economy. See www.scotland.gov.uk/News/Releases/2005/05/20134522 (accessed 19 November 2007).

The Scottish Government (2010) Second homecoming in 2014. See www.scotland.gov.uk/News/Releases/2010/05/25113855 (accessed 15 January 2012).

Therborn, G. (1996) *Monumental Europe: The National Years of the Iconography of European Capital Cities.* Gottenberg: University of Gottenberg.

Thomas, J. (1965) *The West Highland Railway*. Newton Abbott: David and Charles.

Tilden, F. (1977) *Interpreting Our Heritage*. Chapel Hill: University of North Carolina Press.

Timothy, D.J. (1997) Tourism and the personal heritage experience. *Annals of Tourism Research* 24 (3), 751–754.

Timothy, D.J. (2008) Genealogical mobility: Tourism and the search for a personal past. In D.J. Timothy and J.K. Guelke (eds) *Geography and Genealogy: Locating Personal Pasts* (pp. 115–136). Aldershot: Ashgate.

Timothy, D.J. and Boyd, S.W. (2003) *Heritage Tourism*. Harlow, UK: Prentice Hall.

Timothy, D.J. and Coles, T. (2004) Tourism and diasporas: Current issues and future opportunities. In T. Coles and D.J. Timothy (eds) *Tourism, Diasporas, and Space* (pp. 291–299). London: Routledge.

Tnsescu, A. (2006) Tourism, nationalism and post-communist Romania: The life and death of Dracula Park. *Journal of Tourism and Cultural Change* 4 (3), 159–176.

Tourism Framework for Action (2002–2005) See http://www.scotland.gov.uk/Resource/Doc/159188/0043309.pdf (accessed 5 March 2014).

Tourism Resources Company (2006) The Burns journey, development and interpretation strategy. *Scottish Enterprise Network*, Vol. I and II. See www.scottish-enterprise.com/publications/burns_report_for_se_ayrshire_volume_i__the_burns_journey_.pdf (accessed 20 October 2009).

Trevor-Roper, H. (1983) The invention of tradition: The highland tradition of Scotland. In E. Hobsbawm and T. Ranger (eds) *The Invention of Tradition* (pp. 15–41). Cambridge: Cambridge University Press.
Tribe, J. (2006) The truth about tourism. *Annals of Tourism Research* 33 (2), 360–380.
Urry, J. (2002) *The Tourist Gaze*. London: Sage.
Urry, J. (2006) *The Tourist Gaze* (2nd edn). London: Sage.
Valiance, H.A. (1972) *The Highland Railway*. London: Pan.
Van den Berghe, P. and Keyes, C. (1984) Introduction: Tourism and re-created ethnicity. *Annals of Tourism Research* 11 (3), 343–352.
VisitScotland (2008) *The 2007 Visitor Attraction Monitor*. Edinburgh: VisitScotland.
VisitScotland (2009a) Homecoming Scotland 2009. See www.visitscotland.org/events-and-training/homecomingscotland.htm
VisitScotland (2009b) Research and statistics. See www.visitscotland.org/what_we_do/marketing/the_homecoming_story.aspx
VisitScotland (2010) *The 2009 Visitor Attraction Monitor*. Edinburgh: VisitScotland.
VisitScotland (2011) See www.visitscotland.org/pdf/Tourism%20in%20Southern%20Scotland%202011.pdf
VisitScotland (2013a) Scotland the key facts on tourism in 2012. See www.visitscotland.org/pdf/VS%20Insights%20Key%20Facts%202012%20(2).pdf
VisitScotland (2013b) Tourism in Edinburgh 2011. Facts & insights. See www.visitscotland.org/pdf/Edinburgh%20Facts%20&%20Insights%202011.pdf
VisitScotland (2013c) Tourism in Glasgow 2011. Facts & insights. See www.visitscotland.org/pdf/Glasgow%20Facts%20&%20Insights%202011.pdf
VisitScotland Dumfries and Galloway (2009) Historic attractions. See www.visitdumfriesandgalloway.co.uk/seeanddo/historicattractions
Wang, N. (1999) Rethinking authenticity in tourism experience. *Annals of Tourism Research* 26 (2), 349–370.
Wang, N. (2000) *Tourism and Modernity: A Sociological Analysis*. New York: Pergamon.
Ward and Lock (1880) *Ward and Lock's (Late Shaw's) Tourist's Picturesque Guide to Oban, Staffa Iona*. London: Ward, Lock and Co.
Watson, N.J. (2006) *The Literary Tourist*. New York: Palgrave.
Weber, M. (1948) *From Max Weber: Essays in Sociology*, eds Hans Gerth and C. Wright Mills. London: Routledge and Kegan Paul.
Webster, B. (1997) *Medieval Scotland: The Making of an Identity*. London: Palgrave.
Williams, A.M. and Hall, C.M. (2000) Tourism and migration: New relationships between production and consumption. *Tourism Geographies* 2 (1), 5–27.
Withers, C. (1992) The historical creation of the Scottish Highlands. In I. Donnachie and C. Whatley (eds) *The Manufacture of Scottish History* (pp. 143–156). Edinburgh: Polygon.
Wordsworth, D. (1997) *Recollections of a Tour Made in Scotland*. London: Yale University Press (original publication 1894).
World Burns Club (2008) Robert Burns Federation. See www.worldburnsclub.com/begin/robert_burns.htm (accessed 8 January 2008).
Wright, A.S. (2009) Destination Ireland: An ancestral and emotional connection for the American tourist. *Journal of Tourism and Cultural Change* 7 (1), 22–33.
Wright, P. (1985) *On Living in an Old Country*. London: Verso.
Yeoman, I., Brass, D. and McMahon-Beattie, U. (2007) Current issues in tourism: The authentic tourist. *Tourism Management* 28 (4), 1128–1138.
Young, A. (1881) *The Angler's and Sketcher's Guide to Sutherland*. Edinburgh: W. Paterson.

Youngson, A.J. (1974) *Beyond the Highland Line*. London: Collins.
Zuelow, E.G.E. (2005) The tourism nexus: National identity and the meanings of tourism since the Irish Civil War. In M. McCarthy (ed.) *Ireland's Heritages: Critical Perspectives on Memory and Identity* (pp. 189–204). Aldershot: Ashgate.
Zuelow, E.G.E. (2006) Kilts versus breeches: The royal visit, tourism and Scottish national memory. *Journeys* 7 (2), 33–53.

Index